P9-DEW-306

From the Authors of the million copy #1 bestseller
Life Extension, A Practical Scientific Approach

By Durk Pearson & Sandy Shaw

Freedom of Informed Choice:
FDA Versus
Nutrient Supplements

"This splendid book puts us even more in Durk Pearson's and Sandy Shaw's debt. Their 'split label' proposal makes great sense — not as an ideal but as a way to reduce the harm that the FDA is doing to our freedom as well as to our health."
— *Milton Friedman, Nobel Prize Economist*

This book shows you:

- HOW inexpensive nutrient supplements can save over $100 billion in health care costs every year

- HOW the FDA blocks communication of truthful health information about nutrients and foods that results in over 100,000 premature deaths every year

- HOW the FDA is violating our Constitutional rights under the First and Fifth Amendments and why they may be vulnerable to a multi-billion dollar class action suit for damages

- WHAT you can do to help take away the FDA's power to arbitrarily remove nutrient supplements from the market

- HOW to convert our current FDA system, in which the FDA restricts truthful, non-misleading, even lifesaving information, into a system in which it provides information

© 1993 by Durk Pearson & Sandy Shaw

Published by Common Sense Press
P.O. Box 1004
Neptune, N.J. 07753-1004

First Printing March, 1993
Printed in the United States of America

Freedom of Informed Choice: FDA vs. Nutrient Supplements
First Edition
ISBN: 0-9636249-0-3

> Authority intoxicates,
> And makes mere sots of magistrates;
> The fumes of it invade the brain,
> And make men giddy, proud and vain.
> — Samuel Butler,
> an English poet and satirist who lived from 1612 to 1680.

Table of Contents

Toward an FDA that Provides — Rather than Restricts — Health Information

i

Freedom of Informed Choice: FDA Versus Nutrient Supplements

Toward an FDA that Provides — Rather than Restricts — Health Information

Introduction

When we became interested in life extension in 1968, the limit on what you could do to extend your healthy active lifespan was information, because there wasn't much known about aging mechanisms. Now, in 1993, the major limit on what you can do to extend your lifespan is regulatory barriers, especially those erected by the FDA.

In order for the public to benefit from the billions of dollars of taxpayers' money being used to fund research on human aging and aging-associated diseases every year, the government must stop trying to act as the sole decision-maker over the flow of information and products based upon that research. Governments are by their nature slow and inefficient, and every day the FDA's giant information bureaucracy is falling farther and farther behind in its ability to manage the rapidly increasing amounts of biomedical information and farther and farther out of touch with the American public's desire to make their own health decisions, not to have these decisions imposed on them by their government.

Arthur L. Caplan, Director of the Center for Biomedical Ethics at the University of Minnesota, commenting on the controversy over the new tamoxifen breast cancer prevention trial, said that most people "neither want nor expect to live in a risk-free world. Americans are strongly committed to the view that each person must decide what sorts of risks and hazards they want to face in the service of attaining goals they hold dear."

Every year, over one hundred thousand Americans die prematurely and over $100,000,000,000 is added to our health care costs because of the FDA's policies that block the dissemination of truthful information and that dramatically increase the costs and risks of taking a health product to the marketplace. To protect the public from snake oil salesmen, the FDA has become the biggest and most dangerous snake of all.

The easiest course in an inherently unsafe world is for the FDA to say "no" to new information and new products. We think it is time to say no to the disastrous results of this policy. But it is not enough to "just say no." *The question remains: What kind of a system will replace the old system?*

The purpose of this book is to discuss a different approach — *freedom of informed choice* — to replace our present unsatisfactory regulatory system at the FDA. Under freedom of informed choice, the FDA *provides*, rather than *restricts*, information about health products, to help consumers and health professionals to use the interaction between factual information and *each individual's unique risk and benefit value judgments*, to make individual health choices for individuals.

The current FDA policies, with their emphasis on enforcement, paternalism, and coercion, are not consistent with the American tradition of freedom of individual choice and violate basic American civil rights guaranteed under the Constitution, including freedom of speech and of the press. We propose a mid-course correction to bring the FDA into closer alignment with these important American traditions and civil rights.

Chapter 1

The Search for Safety in an Unsafe World

We all want the products that we buy to be safe. Yet, complete safety, or the total absence of risk, is an impossible state that can never be achieved by any means. In any health system, there has to be a tradeoff between the risks of health products and the risks of untreated or inadequately treated diseases. The FDA's failure to approve beneficial health products and truthful health claims is harmful to the public health. Yet, the FDA focuses on the harm done by mistakes in making approvals and not on the harm done by failing to approve. As we discuss in this report, the FDA's failure to approve truthful health claims is the greatest blockade to the prevention of disease in America and is responsible for over 100,000 premature deaths per year and over $100,000,000,000 per year in preventable medical expenses.

Nothing is perfectly safe. Any substance, including air and water, is toxic in excessive amounts. Furthermore, safety is defined, not only by scientific facts concerning the toxicity of health products, but by the subjective personal value judgments that affect the risk/benefit assessments of individuals with a wide range of states of health. The risks of a man crossing the street with a car bearing down upon him are not the same as those of a man crossing the street that is clear for miles on each side. The man at severe risk of being hit by a car while crossing the street might be willing to leap to the side, at the risk of injuring himself, in order to avoid the greater risk of being hit by a car and

4

killed. The risk of injury by leaping to the side would be a foolish and unacceptable risk if there were no car coming. Yet, if a government agency prohibited risky leaping to the side, those individuals about to be run over would face a greater risk of being killed. Who is in the best position to know whether a particular individual is about to be run over? Whose value judgments should determine whether and when to leap to the side? *Whose life is it, anyway?*

We propose an FDA that provides information to health product consumers, to help them make their own informed choices, but does not attempt to substitute its bureaucratic decision-making process for the personal values and decisions of hundreds of millions of individuals (with varying states of health) and their health professionals.

Chapter 2

Informed Freedom of Choice for Nutrient Supplement Purchasers

Some people have asked how informed freedom of choice would work in the nutrient supplement market. They ask, if nutrients are not regulated by the FDA as drugs or food additives, how would they be regulated? How would informed freedom of choice be consistent with safety of and truthful claims for nutrient supplements? How would the FDA provide information to the public?

In the past, the FDA could control the public's access to health information they deemed "inappropriate" for public consumption by restricting truthful health claims by those selling health products regulated by the FDA.

Now, however, biomedical information is becoming widely available to the public through a diversity of sources, including better newspaper and magazine reporting about health related issues and even via direct access to scientific journals and databases (such as the National Library of Medicine's MEDLARS database). The FDA no longer has the choice of being a monopoly on truth, yet FDA Commissioner David Kessler still talks of the FDA becoming the *"sole authority on health and nutrition information."* The FDA is dealing with a public that is much better informed than ever before and the FDA's claims of having exclusive information or expertise is no longer credible, especially since the FDA gives much scientifically unjustified and even dangerous health advice to consumers, including the dangerously false claim that consumers get all the nutrients they need in a good diet and that vitamin supplements have no beneficial effects.

Split Label and Advertisement Approach

We propose a system of informed freedom of choice, in which the FDA acts to *provide* information, rather than *restrict* it, to help consumers make choices. Truthful health claims could be made for FDA regulated products, but products listing a non-FDA approved health claim would have to include a prominent statement such as

- *"this health claim is **NOT** approved by the FDA"*

  and

- *"this formulation is **NOT** approved by the FDA"*

  and

- provide equal space on the label, literature, or advertisement where the claim is made for the FDA to say whatever it wishes.

- Perhaps the unapproved product could have an *easily recognizable symbol*, such as the letters FDA in a circle with a diagonal slash through it, to alert consumers.

If the FDA wants to regain its credibility, it will have to provide information and cite scientific studies to an increasingly sophisticated public.

This would be an excellent time to try out our split-label approach, which we suggested in our #1 million copy best-seller *Life Extension, a Practical Scientific Approach* (Warner Books, 1982). The manufacturer can make truthful health claims on the label; the FDA gets equal space and prominence on the label and can say what it wants. Each can provide scientific citations (nutrient companies are not now permitted to do this) and any other information it deems appropriate. The FDA can give any warnings that it wishes to make, and these will directly reach *every* potential consumer for that nutrient product.

Any consumer who wants to make health choices entirely on the basis of the FDA's advice will be free to do so; in fact, by means of the split-label approach, the FDA's advice on nutrients, right or wrong, will reach far more people than it does now.

Everyone will thereby be warned that *they* (not the government and not society) are responsible for choosing their own information sources and making their own supplement choices. The FDA would find it far more difficult to get away with providing obsolete, false, misleading, and sometimes harmful advice that is out of touch with scientific findings.

We have been told that there is some resistance in the nutrient supplement industry to the idea of a label disclosure that a health claim is "not approved by the FDA."

One possible reason for such opposition might be a fear that some nutrient supplement consumers would stop buying products if they realized that the government didn't control the formulations and health claims. Another reason might be an opposition to any form of government coercion, in the form of required disclosures or anything else, on nutrient labels.

We are sympathetic to those who would prefer that the government have no control over labels, except when there is fraud involved. However, it is simply unrealistic, given the power of Congressional opponents (such as Henry Waxman, John Dingell, Ted Kennedy, and Howard Metzenbaum) to a laissez faire approach to nutrient product health claims to expect complete freedom from government regulation of label and advertisement content. Even with a tremendous public outcry against the FDA, some kind of compromise will likely be necessary in order to get Congress to go along with taking power away from the FDA's current and proposed regulation of nutrient supplements so that there will be continued freedom to buy and sell nutrient supplements and new freedom to make truthful non-misleading health claims.

It is undoubtedly true that some consumers using dietary supplements think supplements are going through an FDA approval process and might discontinue using certain products if they realized the FDA had nothing to do with most nutrient formulations. Those consumers are likely to become more conservative and to act more carefully. We don't think that the nutrient supplement industry can ethically both attack the FDA's regulation of nutrient supplements and hide behind the FDA by hoping that consumers will not find out that the FDA has not approved nutrient supplement formulations and health claims. The FDA quite reasonably does not want the public to hold it responsible for the consequences of people freely using formulations over which the FDA has no control. A label disclosure that a product's health claim or formula is "not approved by the FDA" does not compromise a system of freedom of informed choice but might help to assuage the doubts of those in government and elsewhere who distrust the ability of consumers to make health choices by providing a warning to consumers that these products have not received FDA approval.

An advantage to the nutrient supplement industry of this type of disclosure is that it will further disassociate nutrient supplements from the FDA, showing that good health is quite possible — indeed, much more probable — in the absence of FDA controls.

In one interview that FDA Commissioner David Kessler gave, he suggested that nutrient supplement formulations ought to carry a "not approved by FDA" label disclosure so that the public would not blame the FDA for any untoward consequences of freely available nutrient formulations. We think that his request is a reasonable one and is the only public statement of his that we can recall with which we have been in agreement.

We recently formulated a product for the Life Extension Foundation (an independent organization that we did not establish and over which we have no control) that incorporated many of the above suggestions for label content. The product, called First Amendment Aspirin

Plus™ (containing aspirin, vitamin B-6, and beta carotene), includes a label claim that the product is to be taken
to reduce the risk of heart attacks, a reference to a published paper on results from the Physicians' Health Study
that supports this health claim, and statements that the
product is "not approved by the FDA" and that the health
claim is "not approved by the FDA." We also added a
symbol, the letters FDA in a circle with a slash through it,
as a readily recognizable warning that the product had no
FDA approval.

The Life Extension Foundation had the guts to
produce and is distributing this product. To buy your own
bottle of our highly unapproved First Amendment Aspirin
Plus™ (which might be a collector's item someday!),
phone the Life Extension Foundation at **1-800-841-LIFE**
(tell them Durk & Sandy sent you).

*All profits from the sales of this product will be put into
the Life Extension Foundation's First Amendment Litigation Fund to be used to attack the FDA in Federal courts
over its unconstitutional regulation and prohibition of the
First Amendment free speech rights guaranteed to every
American.*

Forbidden Knowledge about Low Dose Aspirin

The FDA doesn't want you to read this ad.

(advertisement)

FDA Restrictions on Disclosure of Lifesaving Medical Information Kill 100,000 Americans Every Year

Inexpensive Remedy Dramatically Reduces Heart Attack Risk in Major Government Sponsored Research Study

About 1.5 million Americans suffer a heart attack every year. Over 500,000 die. Of that number, at least **100,000** people die prematurely because they are not taking a simple, very inexpensive over the counter drug that has been shown in over a dozen scientific studies to substantially reduce the risk of heart attacks. Yet, the FDA explicitly forbids the drug's manufacturers from educating the public about these widely accepted effects on labels or in advertising. The amount required to provide substantial protection costs only about a penny a day. *The drug is aspirin.*

The first published report on a protective effect of aspirin was in 1948. Many other studies followed. In 1989 the results of the huge Physicians ' Health Study of the effects of low dose aspirin on heart attack incidence were reported as front page headlines in newspapers. The study involved over 22,000 physician subjects, was funded by the government (National Institutes of Health), and was conducted by Harvard University Medical School. *The published study reported that low dose aspirin (an aspirin every other day) reduced the risk of a first heart attack by 44% in men over 50 years of age. (The evidence on the effects of aspirin on women, who were not in this study but have been included in others, suggest similar effects.)*

Recently, Dr. Charles H. Hennekens, head of the Physicians' Health Study, reported additional results from the study that indicate that beta carotene may also provide protection against heart attack. (Beta carotene was included in the study to follow up scores of earlier research studies indicating that it has cancer preventive properties.) In a subgroup of 330 subjects who had pre-existing cardiovascular disease, those receiving beta carotene alone had a 41 % reduction in major incidents (such as heart attack and stroke) compared to placebo, while those receiving both beta carotene and aspirin had a reduction of 100% (there were no major incidents in this group, compared to 17 in the placebo group). The FDA permits no health claims of any kind for beta carotene.

The FDA vs. the First Amendment How You Can Help

The Life Extension Foundation is distributing **First Amendment Aspirin Plus™**, which contains (per tablet) 175 mg. of magnesium buffered aspirin (equal to one half aspirin), 83,000 iu. beta carotene, and 20 mg. of vitamin B6, a nutrient required for cardiovascular health. Durk Pearson & Sandy Shaw designed the formulation for their own use and have also contributed their formulation's royalties to the Foundation's *First Amendment Litigation Fund.*

The label contains the scientifically justified but FDA unapproved health claim about reducing heart attack risk with low dose aspirin.

*Please help fund our litigation with the FDA over freedom of speech and of the press all the way to the Supreme Court. Contribute $25 and receive your very own bottle of First Amendment Aspirin Plus. (*This is less than you would probably pay for the same amount of beta carotene alone in a health food store.) If you contribute $100, we will send you five 100 tablet bottles.

Send your contributions to the:
Life Extension Foundation
First Amendment Litigation Fund
PO Box 229120
Hollywood, FL 33022-9120

Warning: Some people should not use aspirin, including those who are allergic to it, have an active ulcer, have a bleeding disorder or are already taking a prescription anticoagulant. Individuals who have a personal or family history of hemorrhagic (bleeding) stroke or who have uncontrolled hypertension should consult with their physician. If in doubt, ask your doctor.

References: "Final Report on the Aspirin Component of the Ongoing Physicians' Health Study," *New England Journal of Medicine* Vol. 321 No. 3: pp. 129-135, July 20, 1989; "An Apple a Day or An Aspirin a Day?," *Archives of Internal Medicine* Vol. 151: pp. 1066-1069, June 1991; In Rita Ricardo-Campbell's article *"Drug Lag: Federal Government Decision Making,"* (Hoover Institution Press, 1976), she describes (pg. 48), the discontinuation of a proposed 1969 double blind placebo controlled clinical study by Squibb on aspirin for heart attack prevention because the company was discouraged by the many rules and regulations imposed by the FDA, including requiring them to submit to the FDA *all known studies on aspirin.* The company considered this unreasonable scrutiny for a drug that had been used since 1899!

* Results announced at the Nov. 12-15, 1990 American Heart Association scientific meeting in Dallas, Texas.

***Pearson & Shaw have no control over the independent nonprofit Life Extension Foundation.*

Chapter 3

FDA Decreases Safety as it Bans Truthful Health Claims

Low Dose Aspirin Reduces the Risk of Cardiovascular Disease

The FDA prohibits truthful but non-FDA approved health claims for the products it regulates, including foods, nutrients, prescription drugs, over the counter drugs, and medical devices.

This prohibition policy is resulting in the premature deaths and disabilities of over one hundred thousand Americans every year, a tremendous cost to pay for the alleged "safety" provided by FDA regulation.

A good example is low dose aspirin, which has been shown in over a dozen clinical trials (the first of which was reported in 1948), to significantly reduce the risk of heart attack. The Physicians Health Study, published in 1989, was a large (22,000 physician-subjects) and expensive government funded multi-year study conducted by Harvard University scientists, that was intended as a definitive study of the heart attack preventive effects of aspirin. (Another part of the study involved a large human trial of beta carotene's ability to reduce the risk of cancer, as indicated by much prior scientific research — this part of the Physicians Health Study is still continuing, since cancer tends to take longer to develop than acute cardiovascular disease).

13

The experimental cardiovascular subjects were over 22,000 male health professionals taking low dose aspirin (one aspirin every other day) or a placebo over a planned period of ten years. In 1989, the study's scientist-physician authors reported that men over 50 on low dose aspirin had a 44% reduction in the incidence of first heart attacks compared to a similar group of men receiving placebo. The paper noted that there were "significant benefits of aspirin for both fatal and non-fatal events." The study reported no reduction in the risk of death from all cardiovascular causes, however; the study's authors noted that it was not possible to evaluate this due to a very low cardiovascular mortality rate among the physician subjects — only about 15% of that expected for a general population of white men with the same age distribution over a similar period. Because of the low cardiovascular death rate, the study would have had to run until the year 2000 before the effects of aspirin on all cardiovascular deaths could have been determined.

The study, which was planned to run for 10 years, was cut short to about five years by its overseeing ethics committee, which deemed it unethical (because it would have resulted in many unnecessary heart attacks) not to give those on placebo the opportunity of taking low dose aspirin.

These results are widely accepted among doctors and scientists. Despite this uncontroversial, mainstream science, the FDA has specifically prohibited aspirin companies from mentioning this study in their advertising because prevention of first or subsequent heart attacks is not an FDA approved label or advertising claim. (See

Appendix 6 for a copy of an FDA regulatory letter on this subject to Sterling Drug, makers of Bayer aspirin.) No pharmaceutical company is going to spend the huge costs of receiving FDA approval for a health claim for an unpatentable substance (aspirin was introduced in 1899). Each year in America, about 1,500,000 people have a heart attack, resulting in 500,000 deaths. About 40% of those deaths are sudden and unexpected; those people do not know that they have cardiovascular disease. Evidence indicates that most people at risk of heart attack, especially those not under the regular care of a physician, are not taking aspirin for heart attack prevention.

Vitamin C Reduces the Risk of Cardiovascular Disease

Extensive evidence from scientific studies supports the existence of significant disease preventive effects of certain nutrients (most notably, antioxidant vitamins C and E and beta carotene), including a marked reduction in the risks of cardiovascular disease and cancer.

A recently published epidemiological study (where lifestyle or risk factors are correlated with disease incidence or mortality) published by UCLA scientists reported that, in a ten year study of over 11,000 Americans, the men who got about 800 mg. of vitamin C a day (mostly from supplements), lived six years longer than men who received only about the RDA of vitamin C in their diets.

There was a 30% reduction in mortality rate from all causes in men getting the roughly 800 mg. of vitamin C a day compared to men getting 50 mg. a day or more of vitamin C in their diets, but taking no supplements. The RDA of vitamin C (which was set at the level that prevents scurvy in nearly all people) is 60 mg. a day. The women subjects who got the high dose vitamin C lived a year longer than those who received average amounts of vitamin C in their diet, but took no supplements.

These lifespan increases were largely due to decreases in mortality from cardiovascular disease. The study's scientist-authors said, at the end of their discussion of the study,

"...the inverse relation of total mortality to vitamin C intake is stronger and more consistent in this population than the relation of total mortality to serum cholesterol and dietary fat intake, two variables on which strong public health guidelines have been issued over the years."

This study was published in the May 1992 *Epidemiology*, a highly respected, peer reviewed scientific journal. Despite this and many other vitamin C studies demonstrating health benefits for higher than RDA amounts, the FDA permits no health claims for vitamin C other than that it prevents scurvy. [Note: the limited length of this report does not permit us to review some of the important studies on vitamin E and on beta carotene, showing that both markedly reduce the risk of cardiovascular disease and cancer. No health claims for them are permitted by the FDA, either. See "Appendix 1: References and Notes" toward the end of this book for references to studies on the disease preventive effects of antioxidant vitamins (including vitamins C and E) and beta carotene.]

Chapter 4

Reducing Health Care Costs by Preventing Disease

Health care costs are dramatically increasing, yet the FDA stands in the way of a major means for decreasing such costs: reducing the incidence of costly age-related medical conditions (especially cardiovascular disease and cancer) through the use of preventive measures such as taking low dose aspirin and/or antioxidant nutrients C and E and beta carotene.

Senate Majority Leader George Mitchell has recently said that he thinks prevention is the best way to reduce health care costs; we hope that the new President will listen to him. The FDA's ban on truthful claims is contributing significantly to higher levels of disease and their attendant health care costs by reducing public knowledge of the simplest, most easily implemented, and least expensive techniques for disease prevention.

Chapter 5

FDA Blocks Truthful Health Claims

The FDA considers *any* health claims for nutrients to be "mislabeling" and subjects nutrient products with truthful claims to seizure, except for a few recently proposed claims by the FDA that do not include a health claim for antioxidant nutrients C, E or beta carotene! Americans can help reduce their risks of chronic and age-related disease and reduce overall health costs in America through the use of nutrient supplements. The FDA's bias against nutrient supplements is a far greater danger to the health of Americans than the certainty that, under any system, there will always be some incorrect and/or fraudulent claims for nutrient supplements. Those accused of health fraud would, in our proposed system, have to be taken to federal court on fraud charges, where those so charged will be able to defend themselves and be protected with the same Constitutional rights as those enjoyed by anyone else accused of a crime.

Folic Acid and Neural Tube Defects

Hey, hey, FDA, how many kids did you kill today?

The FDA does not permit a health claim for folic acid in foods or nutrient supplement products that "folic acid can reduce the risk of neural tube defects, such as spina bifida." Yet, this is a widely held scientific view. The U.S. Public Health Service (the agency which is the parent organization of the FDA) publicly recommends that all women of childbearing age take 400 micrograms of folic acid daily, about twice what most American women get in their diets (mostly from green vegetables).

Godfrey Oakley, the U.S. Centers for Disease Control's head of the CDC division on birth defects and developmental disabilities, says of the folic acid protection, *"You work all your professional career for something like this."*

The British National Health Service has been recommending folic acid to women of childbearing age for a few years and even supplies them with the folic acid.

Neural tube defects are the number one reason for induced abortions in women who *want* to have children. Yet FDA Commissioner David Kessler said that the FDA is not ready to permit a health claim for folic acid to prevent neural tube defects; products with such a health claim are considered by the FDA to be misbranded and subject to seizure!

Kessler says, in justification of the FDA position, that "The line between benefit and risk with folic acid is apparently quite narrow." He bases this upon the fact that folic acid can mask the symptoms of a vitamin B-12 deficiency, which if untreated can lead to serious consequences.

Folic acid, however, is quite low in toxicity and a possible pernicious anemia problem can be simply solved by adding small and safe amounts of vitamin B-12 to any folic acid supplement or folic acid fortified food. (This will eliminate the possibility of pernicious anemia in all except for a small fraction of individuals, mostly elderly, who do not have enough "intrinsic factor" in their GI tract to absorb vitamin B-12.)

In addition, an advisor to the FDA pointed out that a major study conducted by the Medical Research Council in England that demonstrated folic acid's efficacy at preventing neural tube defects, at a high dose of 4,000 micrograms per day, had as subjects "only" women who had already had a neural tube defect pregnancy. Thus, the FDA is not satisfied with the evidence, while the U.S. Public Health Service, the U.S. Centers for Disease Control, the National Health Service, and many others (including us) are.

In the meantime, 2,500 babies are born every year in the U.S. with neural tube defects and unknown thousands of others are aborted. God forbid, that the FDA should simply permit supplement manufacturers to give the facts to women of childbearing age and let them make up their own minds!

Even Congress (consisting mostly of lawyers) is aware of the anti-neural tube defect evidence for folic acid; in its recently passed Nutrition and Labeling Education Act, Congress *legally required* the FDA to consider allowing the health claim that folic acid prevents neural tube defects. The FDA did nothing, ignoring the Congressional mandate. Rather than providing women with information, the FDA is standing in the way because their policy requires that foods and nutrients with health claims are to be treated as "new unapproved drugs," which requires costly and lengthy FDA approval. No company is going to pay these huge approval costs, which average $230,000,000 and 8-10 years for an average new drug, to get FDA approval to make a health claim for an unpatentable substance.

In the "Comment" section of a Sept. 11, 1992 report from the Public Health Service (see References and Notes in the Appendices at the end of this book) explaining the scientific basis for their recommendation of 400 micrograms a day of folic acid to women of childbearing age, they stated that, until the FDA issues final rulemaking on food fortification and permissible health claims on food labeling, that "further food fortification with folic acid would be inappropriate, and no health claims should be made."

Chapter 6

FDA Mandated Fortification of Foods Versus Informed Freedom of Choice of Supplements

The FDA's approach seems to be, *"All that is not required is forbidden!"* (Infamous Nazi slogan.) We do not see why there should be mandatory (required by law) folic acid fortification of the U.S. food supply in the first place since most Americans, including men, post-menopausal women, and children are not in the targeted population of women of childbearing age. The problem of "overfortification" of foods cannot occur if women who need extra folic acid get it from supplements and do not have to keep track of a running total of folic acid consumed from fortified-by-law foods.

A good example of the problems that can occur when common foods are fortified for large populations, only a fraction of whom actually need the fortified nutrients, are associated with mandatory iron fortification of flour. Processed flour is fortified, as required by law, with several nutrients, some of which (like niacin) are simply being added in amounts that replace what was lost during processing. However, iron fortification goes much farther, with iron added that was never in the unaltered grain; the iron was added as a government public health vehicle for delivering extra iron to those individuals who are iron deficient. However, there is now evidence that iron can increase the risks of cancer and cardiovascular disease, especially in men with excess body iron stores.

A Finnish study published in the September 1992 issue of the peer-reviewed scientific journal *Circulation* followed 1,931 middle-aged men who showed no sign of heart disease at the start of the study in 1984. The data revealed that the men with high concentrations (over 200 micrograms per liter of blood) of ferritin (an iron storage protein in the blood) had twice the risk of a heart attack as the men with lower ferritin levels. Men who typically ate high iron containing diets (such as red meats, rich in iron), had a higher risk of having a heart attack than those eating low iron content diets. The scientist-authors suggest that the stored iron may prove a more significant risk factor for coronary heart disease than total blood cholesterol levels.

Another scientist, Jerome L. Sullivan of the Medical University of S. Carolina in Charleston, theorizes that women may be protected against cardiovascular disease because they don't start accumulating iron until after menopause; premenopausal women lose iron every month during menstruation. Sullivan notes that regular blood donation might result in a similar protective effect by decreasing iron stores. He criticized the routine iron supplementation of foods because, he believes, only those with a medically demonstrated iron deficiency should be taking iron supplements.

Because iron is such a powerful free radical catalyst (uncontrolled free radicals are major causative factors in cardiovascular disease, cancer, several other age related diseases, and even aging itself) we have warned against the use of iron supplements and iron fortified foods for over 20 years. We believe that additional iron should be ingested only if recommended by a physician on the basis of clinical laboratory tests that indicate iron deficiency anemia. Most cases of anemia are not caused by iron deficiency; deficiency of folic acid or vitamin B-12 is a far more common cause.

The potential problems of "overfortification" of foods are avoided when individuals get extra nutrients by taking supplements or special dietary foods. Folic acid supplements of known amounts are currently readily and inexpensively available, though without scientifically justified health claims that could help prevent thousands of neural tube defect births and abortions every year.

A report appeared in *The New York Times National* (Nov. 25, 1992) that an advisory committee of the FDA has recommended that food, most likely flour, be fortified with folic acid to prevent neural tube defects despite concerns (as we discuss above) about a possible masking by folic acid of vitamin B-12 deficiencies, largely in older people. The committee did not recommend that vitamin B-12 be added in addition to the folic acid in order to help prevent the latter problem. Furthermore, the committee said it was generally opposed to health claims on food labels, fearing that claims might be exaggerated and foods might be "overfortified."

As we note above, our approach, in which only the population that needs the extra nutrients takes them in the form of special dietary foods or dietary supplements, avoids the overfortification problem.

In addition, we consider the committee's whole approach to mandatory food fortification, in which they view food as a medication with which to "treat" the public (without getting informed consent, as is always required when scientists or doctors propose to "treat" somebody), to be arrogant, elitist, authoritarian, and devoid of any concern about individual choice in the matter. The Almighty Committee thinks that the public should be "treated" by the government through additions of certain government specified substances to common foods *without even allowing food companies to provide label explanations of the health benefits, if any, of such government mandated "treatments."* The Committee and the FDA seem to think that Americans have no more brains, freedom of choice, or personal responsibility than laboratory rats! We do not think the government has the right to choose anyone's foods or medical treatments for them and, accordingly, we strongly oppose mandatory food fortification.

Just as we were about to go to press, the results of a Hungarian study of the effects of folic acid on neural tube defects in 7540 women about to become pregnant was published *(New England Journal of Medicine, Dec. 24, 1992)*. In this study, the effects of 800 micrograms of folic acid a day combined with modest doses of 11 other vitamins was compared to the control regimen, a trace-element supplement that contained small doses of copper, manganese, zinc, and a very small amount of vitamin C. Pregnancy was confirmed in 4753 women, of whom 2420 were on the folic acid/vitamin regimen and 2333 were controls.

There were no neural tube defect infants born in the folic acid / vitamin group, while there were six infants with such defects born in the control group.

The study's authors note that, in the Medical Research Council Vitamin Study, 4 milligrams of folic acid reduced the recurrence of neural tube defects in women who had had a prior neural tube defect pregnancy and that a combination of folic acid plus other vitamins did not provide a greater protective effect. Nevertheless, the authors note that a synergistic effect of the folic acid and other vitamins in their subjects' regimen can't be ruled out. They concluded, *"...we think that all women planning pregnancy should receive a vitamin supplement containing folic acid."*

In an accompanying editorial in the same issue of *The New England Journal of Medicine*, Irwin H. Rosenberg, M.D., of the USDA's Human Nutrition Center on Aging at Tufts University discusses possible policies based upon the folic acid findings in this and other studies. He suggests that food fortification might be the better policy because "As national policy, the use of supplements has the drawback of often excluding those who have the most limited access to health care, are least likely to comply, and are most at risk."

We have noted some very serious objections to mandatory food fortification above. It is certainly true that there will always be those who will not take a supplement no matter how easy you make it for them, even including giving any woman of childbearing age folic acid supplements at taxpayers' expense by issuing special food stamps that may be redeemed only for nutrient supplements. But the problem of people making the wrong choices applies to countless other behaviors, such as using condoms, or contraceptives, or smoking, or excessive drinking, and/or taking certain drugs during pregnancy. We consider the dangers in a public policy of mandating *treatments*, as opposed to making *recommendations*, to far outweigh whatever good they may do.

We object to the expansion of public policies that, by placing the entire burden for the consequences of individual behaviors upon the public, are destroying the incentive for individuals to be concerned with the consequences of their actions. In the insurance industry, this is called a *"moral hazard,"* that is, an incentive for individuals to engage in riskier, less responsible, more careless behavior than they otherwise would. This is another major cause of out-of-control health care costs.

Chapter 7

Regulating Fraudulent Health Claims

The Federal Trade Commission is legally empowered to regulate advertising claims. The FDA has legal authority to regulate only label content. However, through a pernicious "extension of labeling" doctrine, wherein the FDA deems any advertising literature, even (under some circumstances) books written by authors with no connection to the regulated product, to be a part of the label and thus to be under the FDA's authority over labels, the FDA has actually been regulating advertising claims for the food, nutrient, drug, and medical devices industries.

The FTC has a fairly good record of allowing claims when consumers have reasonable ability to judge the results (for example, a claim that a product grows hair on bald heads), where the product appears to be reasonably safe in the intended usage, and where the product has a money back guarantee.

The FDA, in contrast, has a poor record of allowing truthful health claims and their approval, if you can get it, is generally extremely expensive and time consuming, thus delaying and increasing the costs of health enhancing products to Americans who wish to buy them. Because of the FDA's prohibition on truthful health claims, many Americans are not benefiting from extensive research (much of it publicly funded) on the disease preventive effects of certain nutrients.

We propose that the "extension of labeling" doctrine be prohibited so that the FTC, not the FDA, regulates health claim advertising.

A 1989 FTC report *attacked* the FDA's "scientific consensus" requirement for health claims as too restrictive. The report said, "Unlike the [FDA's] fixed consensus approach...the [cost/benefit analysis] technique will allow some claims that are potentially valuable to consumers but do not yet rely upon undisputed evidence." To support its position, the FTC cited the *FDA's past prohibition on dietary fat and cholesterol information on labels.* The FTC report noted, *"Now that a considerable consensus has emerged on the relationship between fat, cholesterol, and heart disease, it appears that a ... regulatory error, resulting in considerable consumer injury, was probably made."*

A second 1989 FTC report came out just after the FDA had attacked Kellogg's and General Mills for repeating National Cancer Institute advice — that a high fiber diet may reduce the risk of certain types of cancer and that people should be ingesting 25 to 35 grams of fiber daily — in their labeling and advertising for their high fiber Heartwise and Benefit cereals, respectively. In fact, the companies even got the exact wording of the fiber advice and permission to use it from the National Cancer Institute, which said that the cereal companies' statement of their advice on the cereal packages was truthful and not misleading. The FTC report showed that the public had significantly increased its consumption of fiber as a result of the information provided by cereal companies in their advertising and on their products' boxes. Eventually, however, the FDA forced Kellogg's to give up the Heartwise name and the cereal subsequently failed in the marketplace. (See pg. 57 for Heartwise® ad banned by the FDA.)

Companies that make claims which are, in the government's opinion, fraudulent, should have the right to defend themselves in a federal court before a jury, where they will have the right to be represented by an attorney, to call witnesses, and to cross-examine FDA witnesses. The current administrative process, in which those accused of false health claims appear in an FDA "court", where the FDA is judge, jury, and executioner, deprives the accused of these American civil rights, and is a violation of the U.S. Constitution's "Separation of Powers" provision.

There are those who argue that having to go through the federal courts to regulate fraudulent health claims is slow and expensive. However, although imperfect, that process should be compared to the defects in our current system wherein the FDA can ban health claims and health products by decree, without having to prove anything; the current system may *appear* to be less expensive, but only if you do not consider the health costs of the FDA's blocking the dissemination of information about ways to help prevent disease. Current FDA regulation of health claims is a system with tremendous potential for abuse, *because it costs the FDA nothing to say "no" to a health claim;* that abuse is taking place, with disastrous effects upon the health — and health budgets — of Americans.

Chapter 8

A Market Approach to Approval of Health Claims

In 1989 and 1990, there were two private organizations that developed serious seal of approval programs to provide consumers with guides to lower cardiovascular risk food: HeartGuide (American Heart Association) and HeartCorps (HeartCorps magazine). During this period, the American College of Nutrition had endorsed certain brands of vegetable oils and the American Medical Women's Association endorsed a brand of calcium containing orange juice.

The FDA took legal action to shut down all these private health claim approval programs, warning all these private organizations that their label endorsements weren't "appropriate."

Vicki Anderson, communications coordinator for HeartGuide, said (April 9, 1990): "Our understanding is they [FDA] intend to clear the playing field." The FDA claimed that third-party endorsements (anybody other than themselves) "tend to increase consumer confusion and may also be misleading." Through aggressive legal action, the FDA was able to maintain its monopoly on health claims, thereby blocking the dissemination of important truthful information about foods.

The seal of approval programs were not perfect. The HeartGuide program, for example, would require a

$50,000 contribution to the American Heart Association's education fund before a company could be eligible for the seal, thus restricting it to companies that could afford those big bucks. The HeartCorps program would have cost marketers $50,000 for testing of a product by an independent lab. Again, most small companies would have been left out. (Of course, the FDA approval costs of $230,000,000 for an average new drug — defined by the FDA as anything for which a health claim is made — is out of the question for all but a handful of large pharmaceutical companies, whose products must be priced accordingly.)

These private programs were never given the chance to develop new and better programs to evaluate food health claims. The FDA clearly saw them as a threat, as they indeed were, to the FDA's "monopoly on truth" and quickly used their big guns to eliminate them. Considering the very poor record of the FDA in allowing truthful health claims, the entrance of private competition would, in our opinion, be a great step forward to better health and reduced health care costs in America.

Chapter 9

Regulating Safety

The safety of nutrient supplements can be regulated in the same way that the FDA regulates food safety now. Contaminated foods have killed *far* more people than all nutrient supplements combined. Years ago, when hundreds of people died in Southern California from eating contaminated soft cheese, the FDA removed all soft cheese from the market in that area. Later, when it became clear that the contaminated soft cheese came from just one dairy, the soft cheese of other companies was permitted back onto the market. In the U.S., people become sick or die from eating many foods, either because of food allergies (many of which are common) or because of contamination (such as salmonella in chicken). Several years ago in Spain, thousands of people died from eating a contaminated cooking oil. People accept these kinds of risks, since catastrophic incidents of injury and death from foods are relatively rare.

Nothing is without risk, including food. Plant foods often naturally contain carcinogens (including hydrazines in ordinary mushrooms), hormones (such as estrogens in wheat germ) and other toxins, the adverse effects of which may not show up for years. Natural aflatoxin (a mold) contamination in peanut butter and in grains leads to thousands of cases of liver cancer in the world every year.

If the FDA required that foods pass all the safety tests (including expensive clinical trials) that are required for drugs, many foods might be removed from the market (especially foods that the FDA did not approve of, such as sweet or salty snack foods). Overall, there would be fewer food products, and the remaining foods would cost a lot more than they do now because of the costs associated with conducting all the tests to receive FDA approval and of meeting all the continuing reporting requirements. There would be a serious problem of access to adequate amounts of certain essential nutrients in America (in the absence of nutrient supplements), with resulting nutrient deficiency diseases, such as scurvy. For example, vitamin C is found most plentifully in fresh fruits and vegetables. The latter are very expensive even now and would be largely out of the reach of most Americans as every day foods under an FDA food safety approval system patterned after its drug approval system.

Nutrient supplements have been used by scores of millions of people over a period of decades and there have rarely been problems. The most serious one was the EMS incident reported in 1989, in which contaminated tryptophan caused the deaths of 38 people and made about 1,600 others sick. When the EMS problem was detected, the FDA correctly removed tryptophan from the market because nobody knew what was causing EMS; later, scientists found that the EMS resulted, not from tryptophan (an essential nutrient!) itself, but from one or more contaminants in a few batches produced by one company that had changed its manufacturing process. If the FDA had treated this like a case of contaminated food, it would then have allowed the tryptophan produced by other companies back on the market. However, they didn't.

The FDA has never approved of Americans taking nutrient supplements and is now preparing to remove all nutrient amino acids and high potency vitamins, as well as herbs, from the market (announced by Gary Dykstra, Deputy FDA Commissioner for Regulatory Affairs, as reported in the August 9, 1992 *The New York Times*). Whatever happened to individual freedom in America? In the area of health, the FDA proposes to eliminate all of our choice whatsoever.

The FDA does not consider the risks of the alternatives that people turn to when the FDA bans a substance. For example, tryptophan was being used by 15,000,000 Americans before its ban (U.S. Centers for Disease Control estimate) for purposes such as inducing sleep or acting as a tranquilizer. Now that tryptophan is no longer available, many of its former users have had to turn to powerful prescription tranquilizers or sedatives that have their own risks of side effects or adverse reactions. Some commonly used sedatives and tranquilizers, including alcohol, meprobamate, barbiturates, benzodiazepines, and chloral hydrate, can cause death (either directly, as a result of accidents occurring under their influence, or by interactions with alcohol or other drugs), and are potentially addictive. Indeed, barbiturates kill over 2,000 Americans every year.

A good example of harmful effects that can result from legislation that bans or limits access to therapeutic substances without consideration of the risks of their alternatives took place in New York recently:

In 1989, New York state required triplicate prescription forms for benzodiazepines, a class of tranquilizers that includes Valium®, to limit their use and, thereby, reduce addiction to these drugs. There have been similar laws passed in other states. The New York law did result in a sharp drop in prescriptions for benzodiazepines, but there was also a marked increase in prescriptions for alternatives such as barbiturates, that are more addictive, less effective, and more dangerous when taken in overdose. This was reported in a paper (Weintraub et al) in the Nov. 6, 1991 issue of *Journal of the American Medical Association*. The researchers concluded that the New York law may have created more problems than it solved.

In their decision to ban supplements of the essential nutrient tryptophan — in spite of the scientific evidence that the problem was caused by contamination at one manufacturer — the FDA did not consider the safety of the alternatives to tryptophan at all!

Chapter 10

A Market Approach to Product Safety

A good example of how market organizations can evaluate product safety and inform consumers is in the area of consumer electronics. Electronic products, if improperly designed or manufactured, are capable of electrocuting us, thereby injuring or killing us, and can also burn down our homes. Yet, this rarely happens and much of the reason for this is Underwriters Laboratory, a private evaluator of safety. UL has no special monopoly status, unlike government agencies, and provides a seal of approval that has worldwide respect. If the VCR you buy has a UL seal, the VCR won't necessarily provide a clear picture, but you can be quite confident that it won't electrocute you or set your house on fire. Can you imagine how good a job a monopoly government agency, like the FDA, would do in evaluating the safety of consumer electronics products? Just think of how much more consumer electronics devices would cost if companies had to spend $230,000,000 for each device to receive FDA approval, as is the case for the average new prescription drug? (In fact, if you include the costs of the drugs which are *not* approved, the cost of obtaining approval for each new drug is over $600,000,000.)

Nobel Laureate, Dr. Milton Friedman

Chapter 11

Nobel Laureate Dr. Milton Friedman Speaks Out

We asked Dr. Milton Friedman what he thought of the FDA's plans, announced by the FDA Deputy Commissioner for Regulatory Affairs Gary Dykstra, to ban or regulate out of existence (by declaring them unapproved drugs or unapproved food additives) most nutrient supplements and herbs currently available. Dr. Friedman replied,

"The FDA has already done enormous harm to the health of the American public by greatly increasing the costs of pharmaceutical research, thereby reducing the supply of new and effective drugs, and by delaying the approval of such drugs as survive the tortuous FDA process. Any increase in the FDA's authority over anything is a clear and present danger to the nation's health."

Chapter 12

The Health Freedom Act*

The "Health Freedom Act" (S. 2835) was introduced in the Senate in 1992 by Senator Orrin Hatch (R-Utah), while a similar measure in the house (HR 5703) was introduced by Congressman Elton Gallegly. These bills would prohibit the FDA from arbitrarily regulating or banning the sale of nutrient supplements by declaring them to be unapproved drugs or unapproved food additives (the FDA has announced its intention to ban the sale of amino acids, herbs, and high potency vitamins in this way in 1993). They will be re-introduced this year.

The Hatch bill would also allow truthful health claims where there is significant scientific evidence (not necessarily a scientific consensus, as interpreted by the FDA) and would permit nutrient supplement companies to challenge the FDA's ban of a health claim in a federal court. This would go a long way to correcting the FDA's seriously defective and costly policies with regard to nutrient supplements and foods.

There is currently a tremendous political battle raging in the Congress over the Hatch Health Freedom Act. Letters and calls have been flooding into the Congress supporting this bill from users of nutrient supplements (about 25% of American adults take supplements daily, while 50% use them sometimes), as well as health food store and nutrient supplement company owners and employees. If you use nutrient supplements, we strongly urge

40

you to contact your Congressmen by phone, fax, or letter right now.

By requiring the FDA to provide information, rather than restricting it, and prohibiting the FDA from blocking truthful non-misleading health information provided by nutrient and food companies, all Americans will have access to important scientific information with which to evaluate and benefit from the extensive scientific research (much of it publicly funded) on nutrients. It will change an old abusive system wherein an elite of bureaucrats in Washington DC arrogantly take it upon themselves to make the health decisions for hundreds of millions of individual Americans into a new system of informed freedom of choice and individual responsibility. It will help reduce spiraling health costs in America by allowing individuals to focus on actions they can personally take, such as supplementing their diets with antioxidant vitamins C and E and with beta carotene, to reduce their own risks of costly cardiovascular disease and cancer.

* The Health Freedom Act has been re-named the "Dietary Supplement Standards and Consumer Education Act of 1993," sometimes called the Supplement Consumer's Act. Apparently, the word "freedom" in a Congressional Bill is politically incorrect in the United States of 1993.

Appendix 1:

References and Notes

Federal Trade Commission reports critical of FDA regulatory approach to health claims

Colford and Freeman, "FTC Studies Hit FDA on Health Claims," *Advertising Age*, Oct. 9, 1989

Ippolito and Mathios, "Health Claims in Advertising and Labeling: a Study of the Cereal Market," Federal Trade Commission, August 1989

Calfee and Pappalardo, "How Should Health Claims for Foods Be Regulated?," Bureau of Economics, Federal Trade Commission, September 1989

Low dose aspirin reduces risk of first heart attack in men over 50 by 44% in 22,000 subject government funded study:

"Final Report on the Aspirin Component of the Ongoing Physicians' Health Study," *New England Journal of Medicine* 321(3):131-135 (July 20, 1989)

Rita Ricardo-Campbell, "Drug Lag: Federal Government Decision Making" (Hoover Institution Press, 1976)

Beta carotene reduces, by 41%, risk of heart attacks in subgroup of 330 physicians with severe pre-existing cardiovascular disease in the Physicians Health Study:

Data reported by Dr. Charles H. Hennekens, head of the Physicians Health Study, at the Nov. 12-15 1990 American Heart Association scientific meeting in Dallas, Texas

U.S. Public Health Service and U.S. Centers for Disease Control publicly recommend 400 micrograms per day of folic acid to women of childbearing age to prevent neural tube birth defects (the number one reason for abortions in women who want children), but the FDA still won't permit this information in advertising or on labels of folic acid supplements or folic acid containing foods:

Palca, "Agencies Split on Nutrition Advice," *Science,* pg. 1857, 25 Sept. 1992

"Recommendations for the Use of Folic Acid to Reduce the Number of Cases of Spina Bifida and Other Neural Tube Defects," *Morbidity and Mortality Weekly Report* 41(RR-14):1-7 (Sept. 11, 1992); copies of this report may be obtained for $3.00 each from: Massachusetts Medical Society, C.S.P.O. Box 9120, Waltham, MA 02254-9120.

"Folic acid health claim not imminent: Kessler," *Food Chemical News,* Sept. 21, 1992

Czeizel, Dudas, "Prevention of the First Occurrence of Neural-Tube Defects by Periconceptional Vitamin

Supplementation," *New England Journal of Medicine,* Dec. 24, 1992

Disease preventive effects of antioxidants in the news:

"The New Scoop on Vitamins," *Time,* April 6, 1992

Higher than RDA doses of vitamin C reduce cardiovascular mortality and extend lifespan in both men and women:

Enstrom et al, "Vitamin C Intake and Mortality Among a Sample of the United States Population," *Epidemiology* 3:194-202 (1992)

FDA takes legal action to stop private programs to evaluate health claims for consumers:

Meyers, "HeartGuide Legacy: FDA may shoot down other seal programs," *Advertising Age,* April 9, 1990

Walley, "'HeartCorps' Enlists Seal Program," *Advertising Age,* Sept. 18, 1989

Excess iron linked to heart disease:

Fackelmann, "Excess Iron Linked to Heart Disease," *Science News,* pg. 180, Sept. 19, 1992

Sullivan, "Iron and the Sex Difference in Heart Disease Risk," *The Lancet,* June 13, 1981

Excess iron linked to cancer:

Reizenstein, "Iron, Free Radicals, and Cancer," *Medical Oncology and Tumor Pharmacotherapy* 8(4):229-33 (1991)

Nelson, "Dietary Iron and Colorectal Cancer Risk," *Free Radical Biology and Medicine* 12(2):161-8 (1992)

Further information on the health and economic costs of FDA regulatory policy:

Pearson & Shaw, *Life Extension, a Practical Scientific Approach,* "Appendix E: What is the Government Doing About Aging Research?" pp. 564-607, (Warner Books 1982)

Ibid, "Appendix K: References to *Life Extension*," pp. 713-720

Stop the FDA: Save Your Health Freedom, edited by Morgenthaler and Fowkes, 1992, published by Health Freedom Publications, Box 2515, Menlo Park, CA 94026

Gieringer, "Compassion vs. Control: FDA Investigational-Drug Regulation," Cato Institute Policy Analysis No. 72, May 20, 1986

Two examples of recent scientific conferences on antioxidant vitamins and beta carotene in disease prevention (reducing the risk of cardiovascular disease, cancer, and other age-related diseases)

The American Journal of Clinical Nutrition, "Antioxidant Vitamins and Beta Carotene in Disease Prevention," Proceedings of a conference held in London, UK Oct. 2-4, 1989, Supplement to Vol. 53 No. 1, January 1991

The American Journal of Clinical Nutrition "Ascorbic Acid: Biologic Functions and Relation to Cancer," Proceedings of a conference held at the National Institutes of Health, Bethesda, MD, Sept. 10-12, 1990, Supplement to Vol. 54 No. 6, December 1991

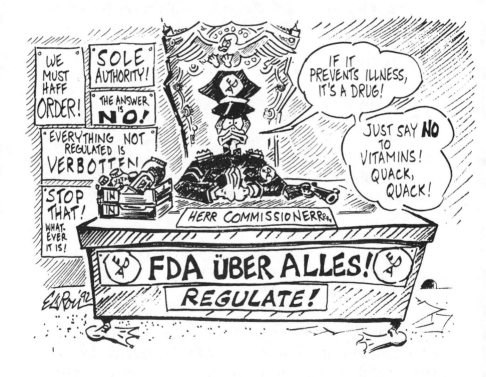

Appendix 2:

The FDA is the Most Dangerous Quack

It is extraordinary that many Congressmen (especially Henry Waxman, John Dingell, Ted Kennedy, and Howard Metzenbaum) express tremendous concern about health claim frauds for nutrient supplements, while the biggest and most lethal such fraud is the FDA's claim that there are no health benefits (other than preventing classical deficiency diseases, such as scurvy) of nutrient supplements, or that health benefits turn nutrients into illegal unapproved new drugs!

A quack claims to have special unique knowledge that makes him or her the sole party capable of judging the worth of a health product. A quack wants you to heed only his or her opinions, and discourages you from seeking information from other sources. These quack attitudes are clearly expressed in FDA Commissioner Kessler's statement that the FDA should be "the sole authority on health and nutrition information."

A quack ignores peer reviewed published scientific studies when the studies contradict their own position, as does the FDA.

A quack is dangerous because he or she might cause you to waste money on a treatment that is unsafe or ineffective but, of far greater importance, because he or she prevents you from learning of and using an effective treatment, as the FDA does.

A quack's worldview frequently revolves around some faulty premise. The FDA's worldview is built on many faulty premises, such as:

- Only the FDA is able to judge the safety of a health product.

- Only the FDA is able to judge the benefits of a health product.

- Only the FDA is able to judge when the probable benefits of a health product outweigh the probable and unknown risks.

- Only the FDA is able to judge the validity of claims made for a health product.

- You can get all the vitamins, minerals, and other micronutrients that you need in a balanced diet.

- Nutrient supplements provide no health benefits other than preventing or treating classical deficiency diseases such as scurvy.

- If nutrient supplements provided any other health benefits, they would become unapproved new drugs, and should be regulated as such.

- There is only one interpretation of the scientific facts — the FDA's.

- The American public will become hopelessly confused if they are exposed to a second opinion.

- Bureaucracy is the only permissible road to good health and scientific truth.

- The FDA, created by Congress, is above the law of the land and is empowered to ignore the First Amendment of the United States Constitution which states that "Congress shall make no law... abridging freedom of speech or of the press."

What does FDA quackery cost? If aspirin manufacturers could make truthful health claims about the cardiovascular health benefits provided by low dose aspirin, about 100,000 premature heart attack deaths or disabilities per year would be prevented in America. If manufacturers of the antioxidant nutrients vitamin C, vitamin E, and beta carotene could make truthful health claims about their products, another 100,000 or more premature deaths from cardiovascular disease and cancer could be prevented. These truthful claims are prohibited under penalty of law by the FDA. This FDA quackery, enforced at gun-point by Federal Marshals, is killing far more Americans every year than perished in the decade long Vietnam War! In addition to the personal and family tragedies (remember, these are dead human beings who leave bereaved spouses, children, and friends), this FDA quackery is also adding at least $100,000,000,000 (that's 100 *billion* dollars) per year to American health care expenses.

PERCEPTION

REALITY!

Appendix 3:

The FDA Versus the First Amendment

"Congress shall make no law... abridging freedom of speech or of the press."

from the First Amendment to the United States Constitution

The Founding Fathers were well aware of what the courts refer to as "commercial speech;" Benjamin Franklin, a printer, even wrote a piece titled "An Apology for Printers," explaining why he had published thousands of advertisements, nearly all of which some people found offensive or wrong.

"An Apology for Printers" first appeared in The Pennsylvania Gazette, for the week June 3 to June 10, 1731. It was reprinted by Acropolis Books, Ltd. in 1973

The Founding Fathers did not exclude either commercial speech in general, or health product claims in particular, from the protection of the First Amendment (which they could have easily done) because they realized that giving the government the power to prohibit speech or writing was far more dangerous than any possible misuse of this freedom could be.

Dr. Benjamin Rush, one of the brave men who signed the Declaration of Independence, argued for an amendment to the Constitution guaranteeing freedom of medical choice, saying,

**"Unless we put medical freedom into the constitu-
tion, the time will come when medicine will organize itself
into an undercover dictatorship. To restrict the art of
healing to one class of men and deny equal privileges to
others will constitute the Bastille of medical science. All
such laws are un-American and despotic."**

> — *Dr. Benjamin Rush, revolutionary war hero,
> physician, and signer of the Declaration of
> Independence*

This proposed amendment was not included in the
Bill of Rights because those who were at the first Constitutional Convention believed that the guarantees of liberty already in the Constitution were so general and strong
that this freedom was already fully protected. Unfortunately, they were wrong.

Dr. Benjamin Rush quote from an article by Kate Joy in Citizens
for Health August 31, 1992 mailing

**Durk & Sandy: "If you could do anything to improve
health in America, what would you do?"**

**Dr. Milton Friedman: "It's very simple. No more
licensing of doctors. No more regulation of drugs. Not of
any kind. Period."**

Here is an all too typical example of how government
regulatory agencies approach our First Amendment free
speech rights:

"The bottom line is very simple: This is against the
law," says Jack Killorin, a spokesman for the Bureau of

Alcohol, Tobacco, and Firearms (BATF). "This isn't a First Amendment issue. You are not allowed to say [wine is] therapeutic and healthful and on sale here today."

BATF-Killoran quote from "Wineries and Government Clash Over Ads That Toast Health Benefits of Drinking," by Carrie Dolan, *Wall Street Journal*, pg. B1, October 19, 1992)

The regulatory agencies seem to believe that all they have to do to escape the First Amendment restrictions on the government is to claim that some kind of speech which they don't like, such as advertising, is not a First Amendment issue: the First Amendment — Void Where Prohibited By Law. When the Beringer wine company asked BATF permission to use part of a *60 Minutes* piece to promote the health values of wine — and made it clear that they considered it to be a First Amendment issue that was ripe for litigation in the Supreme Court — the BATF suddenly had a change of heart and permitted the statement which they described as "truthful, balanced, and not deceptive."

FTC Report Examines Government As a Source of Diet/Health Information

"...there are potential disadvantages to government provision of information, **especially if private sources of information are legally prohibited**. For instance, if government is the sole or major source of such information, **great power is concentrated in one body**." "... if the 'capture' or 'special interest' theories of government explain government behavior (Stigler, 1971) and Peltzman (1976), special interest groups might have undue influence on the types of information developed and disseminated. Similarly, if bureaucratic incentives influence government actions, **these decisions may be excessively risk averse or otherwise unresponsive to changes in science and the marketplace**." (emphasis added) [Note: George Stigler, cited above, received the Nobel Prize in Economics within the past few years.]

"In the nutrition area, for instance, information is usually disseminated through the release of government studies or scientific panel recommendations. These releases are initially limited to one-time reports in the news media, though there is a second round dissemination through the popular press that reports nutrition information." "...the information is generally released in generic form (e.g., 'Increased fiber is likely to reduce the risks of colon cancer.') and not in product-specific form (e.g., 'Product X is a good source of fiber, which may reduce the risks of colon cancer.') Generic information requires that consumers have other sources of information and greater understanding of the issue to turn the information into behavior, ...creating a potential bias towards those most efficient in processing information and those with better access to health information." Thus, food product producers can be an important source of diet/health information that helps consumers to take practical action in response to new scientific information.

Quotes from pp. 19-20 of "Health Claims in Advertising and Labeling: A Study of the Cereal Market" by Pauline M. Ippolito and Alan D. Mathios, Federal Trade Commission, August 1989

Medical Experts Slow to Adopt New Remedies

FDA Blocks/Slows Communication of Information About New Remedies

"Influential medical experts often fail to recommend lifesaving treatments until years after enough clinical data have accumulated to justify their use."

"The findings, which focused on treatments for heart disease, suggest that thousands of lives are lost each year because leading medical authorities aren't keeping up with the ever-growing torrent of research results on new remedies."

This study was published in the July 8, 1992 *Journal of the American Medical Association.*

"One of the most striking examples concerned taking regular doses of aspirin after a heart attack to reduce the chance of a second attack. A majority of medical reviewers didn't begin recommending aspirin after heart attacks until 1986 — a decade after cumulative meta-analysis could have shown that the treatment would save lives... Moreover, a meta-analysis supporting the use of aspirin by heart-attack patients was published in 1980 — six years before most experts finally began recommending it as the standard treatment."

Quotes from "Medical Experts Slow to Adopt New Remedies," by David Stipp, *The Wall Street Journal,* July 8, 1992

FDA's Approach to Health Claims for Aspirin

"Back in February 1988, when reports first surfaced that aspirin use may help prevent heart attacks, the FDA told marketers it was looking into 'whether and how aspirin marketers can utilize this new study.' There's been no word from them — other than a 'cease and desist' or two — since. Now a more definitive study [the Physicians Health Study] has emerged to confirm the earlier reports that aspirin use can be beneficial. And, again, the agency has warned aspirin marketers not to advertise the study's conclusions; it will issue guidelines, it said, this fall. Seems we've heard that kind of promise before."

"While the FDA falls behind in its obligations to consumers and marketers, the American Heart Association is in the process of 'marketing' its new HeartGuide seal for use on products. With marketers — and the public — increasingly looking to such non-governmental groups, FDA will have only itself to blame if its inability to keep up with healthcare developments turns it into a bureaucratic anachronism — a relic of medicine's long-gone 'country doctor' past."

The FDA shortly thereafter took legal action to ban the American Heart Association's HeartGuide seal program. Unfortunately for everyone except the FDA, they succeeded.

Above quotes taken from an editorial "FDA Stuck on Square One" in the August 14, 1989 *Advertising Age*.

An advertisement banned by the FDA:

Kellogg's Heartwise®. **The cereal with psyllium.**

Heartwise® **didn't settle for just one opinion.**

"...Psyllium, when part of a low-fat, low-cholesterol diet, lowers serum cholesterol levels, which I think will be good for most of us."

David J. A. Jenkins, MD, Professor of Medicine and Nutritional, Sciences, University of Toronto

"In my opinion, there are documented studies which reveal the cholesterol-lowering effects of psyllium when part of a low-fat, low-cholesterol diet..."

Robert M. Russell, MD, Professor of Medicine and Professor of Nutrition, Tufts University, Boston, MA

"For the last few years, we have been urging our patients to consume at least 20 grams of soluble fiber daily. Without something like psyllium, it is often very difficult to achieve that intake."

Nikitas J. Zervanos, MD, Clinical Professor, Department of Family, Practice and Community Health,, Temple University School of Medicine

(From an ad for Heartwise® in the June 1991 *National Geographic*. Also contained a coupon for $.50 off on next purchase.)

FDA Attacks "No Cholesterol" Ad Claims

"The Food and Drug Administration expanded its offensive against misleading food labels, demanding that three food manufacturers take no-cholesterol claims off their bottles of high-fat corn oil and canola oil. In letters sent out yesterday, the FDA notified Procter & Gamble Co., CPC International Inc. and Great Foods of America Inc. that the no-cholesterol boasts and depiction of a heart on their product labels are deceptive. While the products don't contain cholesterol, the FDA said, the labels leave the misimpression these products by themselves benefit the heart and overall health. The [FDA] letters threaten the companies with further action if the products aren't relabeled." "FDA Commissioner David Kessler said in an interview that the agency's action is designed to serve notice on manufacturers of hundreds of supermarket items that deceptive claims regarding cholesterol won't be tolerated on products high in fat and saturated fat."

Right. As the FDA appears to see it, consumers are better off with no information at all, than to know whether an oil does or does not contain cholesterol. This suggests that the agency sees no dietary difference between an oil or fat that contains cholesterol (such as tallow) and one that does not (such as corn or canola oils, the relatively low saturated fat kinds that were labeled "no cholesterol" in the disputed ads). It also implies that the FDA thinks American consumers are such fools that they believe all they need to do is use a vegetable oil with no cholesterol and they'd have perfect health! Why doesn't the FDA provide additional information, via a split label approach, if they think consumers need more, rather than unconstitutionally restricting truthful information about a food's nutritional content?

Quotes taken from Ingersoll, "FDA Takes On 'No Cholesterol' Claims," *The Wall Street Journal*, pp. B1-B2, May 15, 1991

FDA Interferes with Dissemination of Information About New Drugs and New Therapeutic Uses for Old Drugs

The FDA has issued "guidelines" aimed at preventing drug companies from "promoting" their products (providing information on new FDA unapproved drugs or unapproved uses of approved drugs), at medical seminars before the FDA has given them approval to do so. The FDA policy statement established criteria that industry-sponsored events, such as symposia and supplements to scientific journals, must meet in order to be deemed by the FDA as nonpromotional and, therefor, not subject to FDA legal action. FDA Commissioner David Kessler said the policy statement is intended to address the "blurring between scientific exchange and pharmaceutical promotion" in recent years as drug companies, limited by strict FDA rules concerning when they may release scientific information about their products, have increasingly turned to nontraditional means of marketing products.

From "FDA Seeks Scrutiny of Drug Industry's Role in Education," by Rose Gutfeld, *The Wall Street Journal*, pg. B3, Nov. 25, 1992

"The Republican-appointed FDA Commissioner David Kessler has spent much of his nearly two years as head of the FDA waging a relentless war against drug marketing. Drug companies have been forced to sign unprecedented consent orders that have halted advertising campaigns, imposed monetary damages, and required extensive counter-advertising and pre-clearance of all new ads. Besides the ever-looming possibility that the FDA might slow pending new-drug approvals, agency officials apparently made offers companies couldn't refuse: Sign or we seize your inventory." "[The FDA has been] distributing copies of proposals to rein in company-sponsored communications, particularly continuing medical education."

"Without communications, drugs aren't delivered to patients. Although traditional medical education and medical journals have an honored place in medical practice, there also is a place for truthful commercial communication..."

Quotes taken from "Battle to Save Drug Ads," by John O'Toole, *Advertising Age*, October 26, 1992) Mr. O'Toole is president of the American Association of Advertising Agencies.

Speech is Speech is Speech

"Speech is speech. It's inconsistent to protect one type and not the other." said NBC News President Michael Gartner about government limits on TV advertising and other limits on commercial speech when he spoke at a celebration of the 200th birthday of the First Amendment. Gartner didn't see much to celebrate. "Speech is not free in this country, nor is the press." Gartner referred to censors in Congress, the Pentagon, the Federal Communications Commission (such as regulations on the content of children's programs and what broadcasters may charge for political ads), on school boards, and at city halls.

Quoted from "NBC Chief: Speech Isn't Free" in the December 17, 1991 *USA Today*.

For further information see Appendix 11, which contains extracts from "Contrived Distinctions: The Doctrine of Commercial Speech in First Amendment Jurisprudence" by Jonathan W. Emord, Policy Analysis No. 161, September 23, 1991; copies are $4.00 each from the Cato Institute, 224 Second St. S.E., Washington, DC 20003

First Amendment Rights and Commercial Free Speech

"In recent years, the U.S. Supreme Court has repeatedly recognized that the right of free speech under the First Amendment to the U.S. Constitution also protects 'commercial speech' (eg., the cases of Zauderer v. Office of Disciplinary Counsel and Virginia State Board of Pharmacy v. Virginia Citizens Consumer Council [references below]. Following such precedents, it can be argued that a food manufacturer has a constitutionally protected right to include in the labeling of a food truthful and non-misleading information about health — or disease — related aspects of the item that may be of importance to consumers"

References to legal cases:

Zauderer v. Office of Disciplinary Counsel (1985) [471 U.S. 626], US Supreme Court

Virginia State Board of Pharmacy v. Virginia Citizens Consumer Council (1976) [425 U.S. 748], US Supreme Court

Above quotes taken from Stephen H. McNamara, "US FDA Rules on Health Claims for Foods," *Trends in Food Science & Technology*, pp. 186-189, August 1991 [Mr. McNamara is with Hyman, Phelps & McNamara, PC, 1120 G St. NW, Suite 1040, Washington, DC 20005]

FDA Ponders First Amendment Issues Raised by FDA Regulations

"Commissioner David Kessler and Deputy Commissioner for Policy Michael R. Taylor are closely studying the First Amendment issues raised by media opponents of their increased regulatory attention to prescription drug marketing. 'These are very tough issues,' Taylor told us 1/13, 'Clearly, verbal speech is not labeling, but verbal indications given for a drug can constitute intended use.'"

The FDA's actions clearly show that any "study" of the First Amendment on its part is for the purpose of finding ways to *circumvent* it.

Quote from "First Amendment issues on drug promotion under review," in the January 15, 1992 *Dickinson's FDA*

The Supreme Court Rules on Commercial Speech

Simon & Schuster Inc., Petitioner

v.

Members of the New York State Crime Victims Board, et al. No. 90-1059. Argued Oct. 15, 1991. Decided Dec. 10, 1991.

In February 1992, the Supreme Court *unanimously* threw out New York's "Son of Sam" statute, which required that an accused or convicted criminal's income from works describing the crime be deposited in an escrow account, which would be made available to victims of crime and the criminal's other creditors, ruling it to be in violation of the First and Fourteenth Amendments. O'Connor, J. delivered opinion of the Supreme Court, in which Rehnquist, C.J.,and White, Stevens, Scalia, and Souter, JJ., joined. Blackmun, J., and Kennedy, J. filed opinions concurring in the judgment.

"Justice O'Connor, J., held that (1) statute was presumptively inconsistent with First Amendment, and (2) statute was not narrowly tailored to achieve State's objective of compensating victims from profits of crime."

"Justice Blackmun and Justice Kennedy issue opinions concurring in judgment."

"Statute is presumptively inconsistent with First Amendment if it imposes financial burden on speakers because of content of their speech. U.S.C.A. Const. Amend. 1"

"Regulations which permit Government to discriminate on basis of content of message cannot be tolerated under First Amendment. U.S. C.A. Const. Amend. 1."

"In context of financial regulation, Government's ability to impose content-based burdens on speech raises specter that Government may effectively drive certain ideas or viewpoints from marketplace; First Amendment presumptively places this sort of discrimination beyond power of Government. U.S.C.A. Const.Amend. 1."

"Constitutional right of free expression is intended to remove governmental restraints from arena of public discussion, putting decision as to what views shall be voiced largely into hands of each of us in belief that no other approach would comport with premise of individual dignity and choice upon which our political system rests. U.S.C.A. Const.Amend. 1."

"...whether First Amendment 'speaker' is considered to be criminal/accused criminal or publisher, [the 'Son of Sam'] law singles out speech on particular subject for financial burden that it places on no other speech and no other income. U.S.C.A. Const. Amend.1; N.Y. McKinney's Executive Law & 632-a."

"Government's power to impose content-based financial disincentives on speech does not vary with identity of speaker. U.S.C.A. Const.Amend. 1."

"Fact that society may find speech offensive is not sufficient reason for suppressing it; indeed, if it is speaker's opinion that gives offense, that consequence is reason for according it constitutional protection. U.S.C.A. Const.Amend. 1."

"If there is bedrock principle underlying First Amendment, it is that Government may not prohibit expression of idea simply because society finds idea itself offensive or disagreeable. U.S.C.A. Const.Amend. 1."

"New York's 'Son of Sam' law...was not narrowly tailored to advance State's compelling interest in compensating victims from fruits of crime; statute was significantly overinclusive, as it applied to works on any subject, provided that they expressed author's thoughts or recollections about his crime, however tangentially or incidentally. U.S.C.A. Const. Amend. 1; N.Y. McKinney's Executive Law § 632-a."

"The Son of Sam law is such a content-based statute. It singles out income derived from expressive activity for a burden the State places on no other income, and it is directed only at works with a specified content."

"...the [New York State Crime Victims] Board has taken the **effect** of the statute and posited that effect as the State's interest. If accepted, this sort of circular defense can sidestep judicial review of almost any statute, because it makes all statutes look narrowly tailored."

[from Justice Kennedy, concurring in the judgment:]

"...above all else, the First Amendment means that government has no power to restrict expression because of its message, its ideas, its subject matter, or its content."

"There are a few legal categories in which content-based regulation has been permitted or at least contemplated. These include obscenity ...defamation ...incitement ...or situations presenting some grave and imminent danger the government has the power to prevent ..."

FDA View of the Supreme Court and the First Amendment

"FDA summarizes the Supreme Court's three criteria for restrictions on commercial speech: 1) a substantial government interest in regulating such speech; 2) a regulation that directly advances this interest; and 3) a regulation that is no more restrictive than necessary. 55 F.R. 5185, citing *Central Hudson Gas & Electric Corp. v. Public Service Commission*, 447 U.S. 557, 564 (1980). But in arguing that its proposal [to regulate food label health claims] *meets* these criteria, FDA discusses only the first two of *Central Hudson's* three rules. There is no mention whatsoever of the third element, the requirement that the regulation be no broader than necessary."

"The reason for this omission is obvious. FDA's proposal, with its requirement that all health claims pay obeisance to PHS [Public Health Service]-reviewed scientific and consumer health summaries, is in no sense 'narrowly tailored to achieve the desired objective.' *Board of Trustees of State University of New York v. Fox*, 109 S.Ct. 3028, 3035 (1989). To the contrary, the proposal could hardly be more expansive."

"If certain health claims can be shown to pose a clear danger of public confusion, then FDA should consider a 'split label' approach as an alternative to some outright ban. Under such an approach the claims would be allowed so long as the food label carried an appropriate counter-claim by FDA."

(Quoted from "Comments of the Competitive Enterprise Institute and Consumer Alert to the Food and Drug Administration on its Reproposed Rule for Health Messages on Food Labels," Docket 85N-0061, by Sam Kazman, General Counsel, Competitive Enterprise Institute, 233 Pennsylvania Ave. S.E., Suite 200, Washington, DC 20003, (202)-547-1010)

Another commercial speech case heading for Supreme Court:

"The three advertising associations last week asked the U.S. Supreme Court to uphold a lower court ruling in a Cincinnati newsrack dispute. The lower court found the newsracks couldn't be banned from city streets just because the racks contained commercial handbills. The American Advertising Federation, Association of National Advertisers, and American Association of Advertising Agencies said the city's ban was unconstitutional. The case, to be argued later this year, offers the court the opportunity to delineate between advertising and free speech."

(from "Groups take stand in newsrack case," *Advertising Age*, June 1, 1992)

Lawyers Wanted

Although there is a great deal of hostility to lawyers these days, good attorneys can be a bulwark of freedom against government tyranny. We believe that the time may be ripe for a multi-billion dollar class action suit against both the FDA as an agency, and against its policymakers as individuals for conspiracy to violate the First Amendment civil rights of scores of millions of identifiable Americans. There have been hundreds of thousands of premature deaths due to heart attacks — about half of which could have been prevented if truthful advertising of the benefits of low dose aspirin and high dose vitamin C had not been prohibited by the FDA. The economic consequences of such a suit could dwarf that of asbestos litigation. The Supreme Court has already ruled that both the FDA and its agents may be sued by citizens in cases involving safety, such as when the FDA approves a vaccine that causes disease in users.

Also see Martin Redish, "Product Health Claims and the First Amendment: Scientific Expression and the Twilight Zone of Commercial Speech," 43 *Vanderbilt Law Review* 1433, 1441-42 (1990)

Appendix 4:

Cartoons

Disclaimer: We make no medical claims for this cartoon appendix (even though some have called laughter the best medicine....oops, forget we said that), because a medical claim would turn these cartoons into a medical device requiring approval by the FDA Expert Committee on Jokes...

We do highly recommend laughter for your political health; it can be one of the best ways to bring down an arrogant political organization with an overinflated sense of its own importance. Remember, LBJ didn't run for President for a second term, even though he would have won, because more and more people were laughing at him and he wasn't getting the respect he expected and wanted. As he said at the time about his decision not to run, "There was no respect; it wasn't fun being President anymore."

"EVOLUTION"

"They stopped doing research! It's safer that way!"

Prevention now is better than
"free" government treatment later.

"PREVENTIVE MEDICINE"
It just seems to make
 a lot more sense!

LETS SEE- MY AD FOR VITAMIN C SHOULD GIVE SOME FACTS. VITAMIN C DOES A LOT MORE THAN PREVENT SCURVY. HMM. WHAT SHOULD I SAY...?

I KNOW - "VITAMIN C PROMOTES HEALING". - NO, NO... I CAN'T SAY THAT. THE FDA WON'T ALLOW IT.

HOW ABOUT "VITAMIN C HELPS PREVENT CANCER AND HEART ATTACKS"? NO - THE FDA WOULD NEVER GO FOR THAT EITHER...

I'LL EXPLAIN HOW VITAMIN C STIMULATES THE IMMUNE SYSTEM.... NAH - THE FDA WON'T PERMIT IT.

THEN WHAT CAN I SAY ABOUT VITAMIN C?

"VITAMIN C PREVENTS SCURVY."

SIGH.

STORY: SANDY SHAW ART: ROBERTA GREGORY © 1981

R GREGORY BOX 3335 VAN NUYS CA 91407

Appendix 5:

The FDA May Owe You Money ...If Your Nutrient Supplement Business is Wiped Out by the FDA's Regulations

"Nor shall private property be taken for public use without just compensation." — *from the Fifth Amendment to the U.S. Constitution*

As we have discussed, the FDA's regulations that ban the provision of truthful health information on product labels and advertising are in violation of the First Amendment to the U.S. Constitution. While the FDA is trying to figure out how to get around the First Amendment, however, we suggest that they hire some other lawyers to start working on the FDA's upcoming problems with the Fifth Amendment's "takings" clause, shown above, because under its provisions the FDA may owe money to business owners whose businesses they destroy with their arbitrary regulations.

The U.S. Supreme Court has written, about the Fifth Amendment's "takings" clause, that "the purpose of forbidding uncompensated takings of private property for public use is to bar Government from forcing some people alone to bear public burdens which, in all fairness and justice, should be borne by the public as a whole." (Armstrong v. U.S., 364 U.S. 40 (1960)).

Unless there is evidence of a safety problem (which can be regulated under the government's "police power" and does not require compensation, with the burden of proof on the government), regulations that stop a company from marketing a nutrient supplement could be interpreted as a "taking" of private property for a public purpose. Under this interpretation, a company so deprived, particularly if it is driven out of business, would be entitled to "just compensation" to pay for its destroyed business (which has a determinable value).

In one recent case, a mining company received compensation of approximately $150,000,000 from the U.S. Court of Claims (which the Supreme Court refused to reverse in Whitney Benefits v. U.S., 1989) for the "taking" of the economic value of its coal mining property, which was destroyed by new environmental regulations. Remember, the purpose of the "takings" clause is not to stop Government from making regulations that take away the use of property and stop economic activity, but to ensure that the cost of public policies is borne by the general public, which (supposedly) benefits from the policies, and to prevent the government from foisting these costs upon a small minority of Americans. It also helps ensure that the government imposes only limited restrictions (those for which the taxpayers are willing to pay) upon people's freedom to use their own resources.

There is reason to believe that, due to the ever expanding restrictions that governments are placing on the use by citizens of their own property, including their businesses, that the Supreme Court will be returning to the definition of "takings" that require compensation that was used for the first 150 years of our nation — until Roosevelt threatened to pack the Supreme Court with several *extra* "Justices" of his own choosing. The Supreme Court has agreed to hear a number of "takings" cases in the near future.

In Connolly v. Pension Benefit Guaranty Corp., 475 U.S. 211 (1985), the U.S. Supreme Court announced that it would not develop a comprehensive policy by which to judge potential "takings" cases, but that it would decide these on a case by case basis. The court gave three factors that would be used to help make such determinations:

1) the severity of economic impact of the regulation on the claimant (is there complete deprivation of all possible economic use or a "mere" diminution of such use);

2) the extent to which the regulation has interfered with distinct investment-backed expectations (would these regulations have been reasonably anticipated); and,

3) the character of the governmental action (is there physical invasion or permanent appropriation of the property).

Note that, if the FDA were, in the absence of convincing evidence of safety issues, to ban entire classes of nutrient supplements, it might destroy businesses manufacturing and selling those nutrients. Furthermore, if the businesses refused to shut down, the FDA would certainly send armed agents to physically invade them and seize products to enforce their regulations, thus meeting many of these Supreme Court criteria for a "taking" that requires "just compensation."

There has been a great recent revival of interest in the "takings" clause, which has been badly neglected by the Supreme Court ever since Franklin D. Roosevelt threatened to "pack" the court if it didn't go along with his policies, many of which could have been challenged under the "takings" clause. The book which started this legal revolution to restore the "takings" clause to its original pre-Roosevelt intent is "Takings" by Richard A. Epstein, James Parker Hall Professor of Law, University of Chicago, published in 1985.

For too long, many of the powerful protections of the U.S. Constitution have languished in neglect. It is time that we rediscover and use them against a government running amok, taking away our property and our freedom.

Other references:

Pollot, *Grand Theft and Petit Larceny: Property Rights in America*, See, for example, pp. 86-90 "The Nature of Regulatory Takings," Pacific Research Institute for Public Policy, 177 Post St., San Francisco, CA 94108 (415-989-0833; FAX 415-989-2411)

Moore, "Just Compensation," *National Journal*, June 13, 1992

Chuck Weller, "Just Compensation for the Regulatory Taking of Mining Claim Property Rights," *California Mining Journal*, November 1992

Crovitz, "Judging Whose Beach Fronts, Wetlands, and Junk Bonds," *The Wall Street Journal*, March 4, 1992

Richard A. Epstein, *Takings: Private Property and the Power of Eminent Domain*, Harvard University Press, 1985 (This was the book waved around by Senator Joseph Biden during the Clarence Thomas Confirmation Hearings; Biden wanted to know whether

Thomas agreed with the legal philosophy in the book which, said Biden, would destroy government regulation as we know it. Hear, hear!)

Appendix 6:

A Regulatory Letter Sent by the FDA to Sterling Drug, Inc., Makers of Bayer Aspirin, Prohibiting the Dissemination on Labels or in Advertising to the Public of Information About the Heart Attack Preventive Effect of Aspirin. [See next 3 pages.]

DEPARTMENT OF HEALTH & HUMAN SERVICES   Public Health Service

MAR 3 0 1988

Food and Drug Administration
Rockville MD 20857

CERTIFIED MAIL
RETURN RECEIPT REQUESTED

REGULATORY LETTER

Robin D. Mills
President
Starling Drug, Inc.
90 Park Avenue
New York, New York 10016

Ref: 88-HFN-312-1

Dear Mr. Mills:

This letter is in reference to the recent distribution of a 28-day " CALENDAR
PAK" of "GENUINE BAYER ASPIRIN" caplets (325mg) by your firm to the
general public. Such product bears labeling direct to the consumer for use in the
prophylaxis of myocardial infarction (MI).

On October 16, 1985, the agency's Division of OTC Drug Evaluation (HFN-210)
issued a "feedback" letter to Edward J. Hiross, Ph.D. in response to your firms's
submissions of comments and data to support amending the "Professional
Labeling" section of the OTC Advisory Review Panel's report on OTC Internal
Analgesics, published in the Federal Register of July 8, 1977. Attached to that
letter were guidelines for "professional labeling" for aspirin tablets, 325 mg. for use
in reducing the risk of death and/or non-fatal myocardial infarction in patients with
a previous infarction or unstable angina pectoris. As you know, due to safety
concerns, such an intended use for "GENUINE BAYER ASPIRIN" is not suitable
for the laity without the supervision of a physician. The "feedback" letter advised
that such labeling "...may be provided to health professionals only and not to the
general public...", and that it "...may not appear on OTC aspirin products...". The
"feedback letter allowed for immediate dissemination of this information to health
professionals prior to the publication of a Tentative Final Monograph for OTC
Internal Analgesics.

The specific design of the referenced packaging, and certain labeling statements
and statements made in the promotion and advertising, such as those that follow,
represent and suggest to the consumer that "GENUINE BAYER ASPIRIN" is
useful in the prevention of heart attack:

28-day "CALENDAR PAK":
  o   "For patients following a doctor prescribed daily regimen of aspirin."

82

- o "For patients who have been directed by their physician to take one aspirin a day."

Other Accompanying labeling:

- o "...Introducing The BAYER Aspirin Calendar Pak...A convenient daily reminder for patients on a doctor-prescribed regimen of one aspirin a day for heart attack prevention..."

- o "...BAYER Aspirin is the No. 1 aspirin brand recommended by physicians for MI prophylaxis..."

- o "...Nearly three million Calendar Pak 7-day samples have already been distributed to physicians as part of an extensive program promoting the benefits of BAYER Aspirin for MI prophylaxis..."

- o "...Extensive advertising on television, radio, and in major magazines is informing consumers about the role of BAYER Aspirin in preventing MI..."

- o "...this past tuesday (sic) the F.D.A. announced that an aspirin every other day will reduce heart attack risk by 47%... In patients who have had one attack and at risk of another doctors are now prescribing an aspirin per day...that is where this calendar pack comes in..."

As defined under 21 CFR 201.128 such statements clearly communicates to consumers an "intended use" in the prophylaxis of MI. Our primary concern is that such labeling may encourage inappropriate self-medication by the lay public with potentially serious adverse health results.

In view of the above, it is our opinion that "GENUINE BAYER ASPIRIN" in the 28-day "CALENDAR PAK" is in serious violation of our Federal Food, Drug, and Cosmetic Act (Act) as follows:

SECTION   BRIEF DESCRIPTION

502(f)(1)   The article, "GENUINE BAYER ASPIRIN" in the 28-day "CALENDAR PAK", is misbranded in that the labeling fails to bear "adequate directions for use" (21 CFR 201.5) for the laity for "intended use" (21 CFR 201.128) in the prophylaxis of myocardial infraction.

We request that you reply within ten (10) days of your receipt of this letter stating the action that you will take to discontinue the marketing and/or distribution of the referenced articles and use of the misbranding labeling. We also would be willing to review what labeling revisions, if any, that you believe would bring the product into compliance.

If corrective action is not promptly undertaken, the Food and Drug Administration is prepared to initiate legal action to enforce the law. The Federal Food, Drug, and Cosmetic Act provides for seizure of illegal products and/or injunction against the manufacturer and/or distributor of illegal products (21 U.S.C. 332 and 334). Your reply should be directed to this office.

Sincerely yours,

John M. Taylor
Associate Commissioner
for Regulatory Affairs

Appendix 7:

Resources

Some nutrient advocacy and lobbying groups:

Here are three advocacy groups for nutrient supplement users with which we are in contact and that we think
are worthy of support. They are doing a good job in
keeping us informed of Congressional progress toward
passage of the Hatch Health Freedom Act and of organ-
izing letter writing campaigns to that end. Any of these
groups can tell you who your Congresscritters are and how
to write to them. There are other advocacy groups with
which we are not in contact. We welcome them to write
us care of this book's publisher for inclusion in any later
printings.

Nutritional Health Alliance (NHA), PO Box 267,
Farmingdale, NY 11735, (800) 226-4NHA; NHA Action
Center, 5910 N. Central Expressway, Suite 760, Dallas,
Texas 75206, (800) 226-4NHA, FAX (214) 891-6115

National Council for Improved Health (NCIH), Box
528, Gainesville, VA 22065, (703) 754-0228, FAX (703)
754-4324

Citizens for Health, PO Box 368, Tacoma, WA 98401,
(206) 922-2457; FAX (206) 922-7583

Tips On Lobbying For Health Freedom

by a Washington Insider

What can you do yourself to help defeat the FDA's assault on nutritional supplements? The best way is to support the passage of The Supplement Consumer's Act by Congress, sponsored by Senator Orrin Hatch (R-UT) and Congressman Bill Richardson (D-NM). This bill will save over $100 billion in health care costs and hundreds of thousands of lives a year — simply by putting an end to FDA tyranny over the nutrient supplement industry. (Now you can see why the FDA is called the Federal Death Administration.)

But how best to do this? It is not by writing your Congressman in Washington a letter. The key to effective lobbying by yourself is to take to heart Tip O'Neil's famous observation: *"All politics are local."* Leave lobbying in Washington to the paid professionals. You should concentrate on your Congressman's local district office right where you live.

First, call Sen. Hatch's office at 202/224-5251 or Rep. Richardson's at 202/225-6190, and request a copy of the bill be mailed to you. Then, with the bill in hand, call your Congressman's office right in your district and ask to speak to the staffer who handles health-related issues for the Congressman. [Information about who your Congressman is can be found in the Federal Government section of the Blue or Yellow Pages of your local telephone directory.] Ask him if the Congressman is a cosponsor of the bill and/or supports it. Be friendly and courteous. Explain to him or her why you think his boss

86

should vote for this bill. Find out what his boss's concerns and reservations are, and discuss them. Try to develop a relationship; call every couple of weeks for an update; pay the staffer a visit and talk to him personally. Congressmen almost always vote how their staff recommends. *Convincing the relevant staffer in the local district office is the most sure fire method to get a Congressman to vote your way.*

For added pressure, see if you know any of the Congressman's principal campaign contributors. To get the major ($200 and up) contributor list for any Congressman, call the Washington office of a large national organization to which you may belong or call any of the organizations listed on page 85 for possible suggestions. Ask the organizations if they could send a researcher to the Congressional Office of Records and Registration in the Longworth Office Building, Room 1036. It should take less than an hour to find the donor list on microfiche and copy it. Offer to pay copying costs and for the researcher's time.

Zero in on those listed who gave the maximum ($1000 per campaign). If you know any of them, talk to them about the bill and get them to personally call the Congressman (who always takes calls of his biggest contributors!). Use any other prominent local connections you may have, such as the head of your Chamber of Commerce, from whom your Congressman would take a call. Understanding that politics really is local will enable you to persuade your Congressman to vote for a healthier and longer-living America.

(PS: These methods are more effective on Congressmen than Senators, whose constituency is state-wide and less local, and whose term is for six years, not just two. But if you can apply them to your Senator, don't hesitate to do so!)

Information on disease prevention with nutrients and other health information:

Searches of biomedical and scientific databases (including the National Library of Medicine's MEDLARS database):

Want your facts straight from the scientific papers, rather than as "interpreted" by the FDA? Help yourself to some forbidden knowledge!

This is the search service that we use ourselves. We let Life Services do our literature searches, even though we have the capability to do it ourselves, because they have far more experience. Our books, listed below, both contain information about MEDLARS: how to access it and how to use the information. Life Services can be contacted at (908) 922-0009 voice, (908) 922-5329 fax [see ad on next two pages].

Our books:

Life Extension, a Practical Scientific Approach (Warner Books, 1982)
The Life Extension Companion (Warner Books, 1984)
Both of these books and many of our articles are available from Life Services Supplements, (800) 542-3230.
Our health letter, *The Durk Pearson & Sandy Shaw Life Extension Newsletter. Back issues, published between March 1988 and June 1991 are in limited supply. The newsletter will resume regular publication early in 1993. If interested in subscribing, write the publisher at Common Sense Press at P.O. Box 1004, Neptune, NJ 07753-1004.*

Looking For High-Quality Biomedical Knowledge?

Ask for the MEDLARS BIOMEDICAL DATABASE listing
of more than 1,500 research reports from the
National Library of Medicine's MEDLARS Database,
the world's largest biomedical source.
Searches also available from Dutch-situated EMBASE,
with 3 times as many Japanese journals
and many smaller publications, the
PHYSICIAN'S DATA QUERY diagnosis and
treatment database as well as many others.

Existing searches available on:
Cancer, Heart Disease, Nutrients, Medicines,
Diagnostics, Treatments, Therapies. Priced from $19.95.
Updates priced from $19.95 (up to 2 full years);
Original searches from $40
Specific and general subjects. No topic is too unusual.
Clinical trials ... latest information.

Call (908) 922-0009
FAX: (908) 922-5329

BIOMEDICAL ABSTRACT SEARCH SERVICE

Biomedical knowledge is expanding so rapidly that most health care
practitioners find it difficult to keep pace with the latest breakthroughs in
their fields. Good News! Up-to-the-minute information appearing in
professional journals has been abstracted and is readily available to you.
Now, with the **Life Services Abstract Search Service**, our computer
network becomes your research assistant. We can provide you with
worldwide computer-generated abstracts of biomedical journal articles
from the National Library of Medicine **MEDLARS** system, the Dutch
Excerpta **EMBASE**, the National Cancer Institute's **PHYSICIAN DATA
QUERY** (PDQ) diagnosis and treatment database, and many others.
These databases access well over 10,000 primary scientific journals
(some of which go back 24 years or more) and other sources, to answer
your biomedical questions.

WHO NEEDS A BIOMEDICAL SEARCH?*

Anyone interested in getting the most up-to-date information concerning a health question. You don't need to be a health care professional.

WHAT CAN A BIOMEDICAL SEARCH PROVIDE?

The right questions to ask when you need to make a decision. The names and affiliations of top experts and researchers in your area of interest.

- The latest treatments for specific health problems
- The interactions between medication, nutrients, and foods
- Information to plan a preventative health program
- Supporting knowledge for a supplement program
- Locations of the best treatment centers for specific ailments
- Data to construct and implement a personal exercise program

HOW TO OBTAIN AN ABSTRACT SEARCH*

Tell us what your area of inquiry is and we will initiate a computer search of the **MEDLARS** system. The results will be a computer printout of useful source information. Each article includes the Title, Author, Source and usually a brief statement which is the **Abstract** (summary) of the article's contents. The number of abstracts depends on both the number of articles written on the subject, and how narrowly you define your search topic. The search proceeds from a general subject limited by qualifying items. You provide us with the subject and the qualifiers, or just a specific question and allow us to define the search parameters. Please allow 10 days to receive your search.

The cost for this service is $40 for up to a 40 page report (usually about 100 abstracts), and $0.20 for each additional page, plus shipping & handling of $3.75 (if you need extra fast service or shipping, please call for a quote). If you have any questions, please call (908) 922-0009 or fax (908) 922-5329.

Please Note: MEDLARS abstracts vary in complexity and do require some effort. They are best used in conjunction with your health care professional. No refunds. All sales final.
*As mentioned in **Durk Pearson & Sandy Shaw's** *Life Extension Newsletter* ™

Appendix 8: Warning to Politicians —Ignorance may be hazardous to your political health;

Americans overwhelmingly support health claims for vitamins, as shown in new public opinion poll

The Nutritional Health Alliance Action Center (5910 N. Central Expressway, Suite 760, Dallas, Texas 75206; 1-(800)-226-4NHA, FAX (214)891-6115) recently commissioned a national public opinion poll to determine the attitude of Americans towards dietary supplements. The poll was conducted by a professional public opinion poll conducting firm Yankelovich Clancy Shulman. Interviews with 502 adult Americans were conducted by telephone on September 10-13, 1992. The sampling error is +/- four percent. Here are the results:

1. Do you personally use vitamins, minerals or herbs on a regular basis?

Yes 46%

No 53%

Not sure 1%

2. If scientific evidence shows that vitamins, minerals and herbs are safe and can help prevent disease, do you think vitamin manufacturers should be able to make truthful health claims for their products, or not?

Yes 85%

No 5%

Not sure 10%

3. If scientific evidence shows that vitamins, minerals and herbs are safe and can help prevent disease, do you think people should have to get a prescription from a doctor to buy these nutritional products, or not?

Yes 13%

No 82%

Not sure 5%

4. As long as vitamins, minerals and herbs are safe and beneficial, do you think people should be able to choose the strength or potency of these nutritional products?

Yes 63%

No 27%

Not sure 10%

5. Do you agree or disagree with this statement: "Consumers should be able to purchase dietary supplements, and companies should be free to sell these products, so long as the labeling and advertising is truthful and non-misleading and there exists a reasonable scientific basis for product claims"?

Agree 89%

Disagree 8%

Not sure 3%

6. Do you think the Food and Drug Administration should be able to classify vitamins, minerals and herbs as drugs solely because a truthful health claim is made in the product's advertisement or its label?

Yes 24%

No 68%

Not sure 8%

7. Where safety is not an issue, do you think the Food and Drug Administration should or should not be allowed to classify vitamins, minerals and herbs as drugs solely because of a nutritional product's strength or potency?

Allowed 22%

Prevented 70%

Not sure 8%

Appendix 9:

Comments of the Competitive Enterprise Institute and Consumer Alert to the FDA's Reproposed Rule for Health Messages on Food Labels

In Appendix 3 on "The FDA Versus the First Amendment," we included an excerpt of some comments sent to the FDA on its proposed rules on health labels during the period of public comments. Since these comments, submitted by the Competitive Enterprise Institute and Consumer Alert, provide a well written and easily understood objection to the FDA's labeling rules on First Amendment grounds, we include it here. This is not only a severe criticism of the FDA's approach, but provides a Constitutional basis for an attack on the FDA in the courts.

The Competitive Enterprise Institute (CEI) is a non-profit organization that promotes free-market approaches to regulation, such as our "split label" labeling and advertising proposal. CEI's scholars write informative articles and editorials for a wide range of newspapers, magazines, and law and economics journals and also discuss these issues on television and radio. They litigate regulatory agencies on Constitutional grounds on selected issues and have won some cases (see the descriptions of their work at the end of this appendix).

CEI's "Death by Regulation" Project, to which we have donated over $1,000, is dedicated to attacking regulations, such as those of the FDA, that kill people. Their articles attacking the FDA emphasize the *costs* (in terms of excess deaths) of the FDA's policies. If more people understood these immense lethal costs, we are sure they would oppose the policies that are responsible. We encourage you to contribute a tax-deductible donation to the Competitive Enterprise Institute's "Death by Regulation" project. Tell them we sent you!

Publications available from CEI, 233 Pennsylvania Ave. SE, Suite 200, Washington, DC 20003 (prices include shipping):

"Death by Regulation" (originally published in *Regulation* magazine) by Sam Kazman, General Counsel of the Competitive Enterprise Institute, $3.00

"Deadly Overcaution: FDA's Drug Approval Process" by Sam Kazman (originally published in *The Journal of Regulation and Social Costs*), $2.00. Although this piece describes the deadly effects of the FDA's slow drug approval process, the same principles apply to the FDA's slow approval of everything, including health claims. Remember that for years the FDA wouldn't allow any information about cholesterol and fats on food labels. Now it is requiring it and acts as though it discovered cholesterol and fats in the first place!

CEI v. National Highway Traffic Safety Administration, $2.00

A federal court finds that a safety agency concealed the lethal effects of a major program through the use of "fudged" data, "statistical legerdemain," and "bureau-

95

cratic mumbo-jumbo." This is a case won by CEI in the courts and is a delightful attack on regulations that kill people. (U.S. Court of Appeals for the D.C. Circuit)

DEATH BY REGULATION

is one of today's most serious threats to public health and private liberty. Much has been written about the economic cost of government overregulation, but there is a human toll that is far less appreciated. When new technologies are halted and new products are restricted, the result is not only wasted dollars, but often lost lives as well. Unfortunately, in the current political process, victims of Death by Regulation are too easily ignored by politicians, journalists, and bureaucrats. For practical purposes, they are, sadly, too often invisible.

THE COMPETITIVE ENTERPRISE INSTITUTE

is leading the fight against Death by Regulation. CEI is a nonprofit, taxexempt activist organization committed to promoting individual freedom and to exposing the true costs of overregulation. In areas ranging from medical drug regulation to restrictions on energy use and new technology, CEI is reframing policy debates with winning arguments.

FOR EXAMPLE: For more than a decade, the federal new car fuel economy program (known as CAFE) has restricted the availability of large cars in the name of fuel efficiency. The economic cost of this program, in terms of lost jobs and higher prices, is well established; but its human cost is only now becoming recognized. CAFE kills! Large cars are more crashworthy than small cars. Because CAFE limits large car production, it increases highway fatalities.

You'd think that the National Highway Traffic Safety Administration, which runs CAFE, would try to reduce this lethal effect. Instead, however, NHTSA did its best to conceal this issue from the public; as a "safety" agency, NHTSA simply could not admit that it was killing people.

In 1992, CEI won a federal court decision exposing this coverup. In blunt language, the court found that NHTSA had "fudged" the data, engaged in "statistical legerdemain," and taken a "let them eat cake" attitude towards consumers. The court concluded:

> "When the government regulates in a way that prices many of its citizens out of access to ... safety, it owes them reasonable candor. If it provides that, the affected citizens at least know that the government has faced up to the meaning of its choice. [Administrative law] ensures this result and prevents officials from cowering behind bureaucratic mumbo jumbo." From the decision of the U.S. Court of Appeals in **Competitive Enterprise Institute v. National Highway Traffic Safety Administration**, 956 F.2d 321 (D.C. Cir. 1992)

Get Our Materials
Support Our Work
For further information, please contact:

THE COMPETITIVE ENTERPRISE INSTITUTE
233 Pennsylvania Avenue SE, Suite 200
Washington, D.C. 20003
(202) 547-1010

CEI THE FREE MARKET LEGAL PROGRAM

The Free Market Legal Program was launched by CEI in the fall of 1986 to carry the battle for economic rights into the legal arena The Legal Program's basic objective is to develop new tools for challenging government regulations, and to use these tools in administrative and court actions to better balance the public policy debate. The Legal Program focuses on restoring the rights of property and of contract rights that are basic to a free society, but which current public policies relegate to secondary status.

These objectives are advanced by the Legal Program's *Death By Regulation* project, which identifies the unrecognized health and safety costs of government regulatory programs. Health and safety are frequently the rationale for expanding government programs. By showing how such programs often produce the very opposite of their claims, the *Death By Regulation* project creates a new basis for legal challenges. It also advances public understanding of how government programs fail and how markets work. Our goal is a more balanced public understanding of private versus political approaches. Were the public to view government with even a fraction of the distrust that it currently has for markets, civic education would be greatly advanced.

The Legal Program selects issues and cases on the basis of their importance as policy and precedent, and on the likelihood that CEI can make a significant contribution. We avoid controversies in which the promarket viewpoint is already adequately represented by industry or by other public interest groups. Unless exceptional circumstances exist, we also avoid *amicus* work Experience has shown that such friend of the court briefs, especially at the Supreme Court level, rarely contribute to the final outcome. Finally, CEI does not hire outside counsel to do its legal work; we do it ourselves, at a fraction of the cost.

Growth in CEI's Legal Program is expected. With sufficient funding, our legal work will maintain and increase its focus on FDA reform, rent control, and lethally counter productive fuel efficiency standards imposed on automobile manufacturers and drivers. We also intend to once again challenge restrictions of the freedom of speech in the marketplace.

CEI recognizes that the viability of any market depends upon the free flow of information and that the First Amendment protects the rights of consumers and producers of commercial speech, as well as political speech. In addition, we will seek to expand our project to restore property rights into the field of environmental law.

The Free Market Legal Program has made significant progress toward achieving its goals. Your help would enable CEI to sustain that progress.

COMPETITIVE ENTERPRISE INSTITUTE
233 Pennsylvania Ave. SE, Suite 200, WASHINGTON, DC 20003
PHONE: (202) 547-1010

COMMENTS OF THE COMPETITIVE ENTERPRISE INSTITUTE AND CONSUMER ALERT

TO THE FOOD AND DRUG ADMINISTRATION

ON ITS REPROPOSED RULE FOR HEALTH MESSAGES ON FOOD LABELS

Docket 85N-0061

The Competitive Enterprise Institute (CEI) and Consumer Alert hereby submit these comments on the Food and Drug Administration's (FDA) reproposed rule for health messages on food labels. 55 F.R. 5176 (Feb. 13, 1990)

INTRODUCTION

CEI is a nonprofit organization devoted to promoting free market approaches to regulatory issues. It engages in analysis, education and advocacy on such issues of public interest as agricultural policy, medical drug regulation, and commercial speech. Consumer Alert is a nonprofit organization of over 6,000 members that attempts to defend and expand consumer choice in the marketplace and to increase public awareness of the hidden costs of government regulation. CEI and Consumer Alert submitted joint comments on the advance notice of proposed rulemaking that preceded this reproposal.

SUMMARY OF FDA'S PROPOSED RULE

FDA's reproposed rule essentially bans any health message on a food label unless there is "significant agreement ... among qualified experts that the statement is supported by" "the totality of publicly available scientific evidence". The message must also be "consistent with generally recognized medical and nutritional principles" and it must be "based on and consistent with the conclusions set forth in an applicable scientific summary and consumer health message summary accepted by FDA." Proposed amendments to 21 C.F.R. 101.9(i)(1).

Two studies, the Surgeon General's 1988 Report on Nutrition and Health and the National Research Council's "Diet and Health: Implications For Reducing Chronic Disease Risk" (National Academy of Sciences 1989), are characterized as "represent[ing] the most generally agreed upon scientific basis for health messages" and are proposed as a standard for the scientific consensus required under this rule. 55 F.R. 5178, 5181. On the basis of these two reports, FDA sets out six areas in which it might consider health messages to be appropriate: 1) calcium and osteoporosis; 2) sodium and hypertension; 3) lipids and cardiovascular disease; 4) lipids and cancer; 5) fiber and cancer; and 6) fiber and cardiovascular disease. Health claims on other topics might be allowed as scientific knowledge advances, but only after the development of FDA-approved scientific summaries and consumer health message summaries on these topics.

A Public Health Service Committee on Health Messages (PHS), composed of representatives from FDA and four other government units, would have advisory power over the health message review process, including the drafting of the scientific and consumer summaries and of model label statements.

NOW THAT FDA ADMITS TO REGULATING SPEECH, IT SHOULD PAY SOME ATTENTION TO WHAT THAT ENTAILS

In our prior submission to FDA on this issue (Docket 89N-0226), we stated that:

"the issue of whether consumers can be 'trusted' with information is not a matter for FDA to decide, for it has already been decided by the Framers of the Constitution in the protection that they afforded to speech. FDA appears to have drafted its proposal in total ignorance of this constitutional policy. Nowhere in the FDA proposal does one find the slightest appreciation by the agency that it is regulating speech and not some garden-variety economic activity." CEI Comments at 5 (Jan. 5, 1990).

FDA has altered this approach only marginally in its reproposed rule. While finally acknowledging that it is regulating speech, the agency has deliberately ducked the task of showing that its proposal meets the legal requirements for such regulation.

FDA summarizes the Supreme Court's three criteria for restrictions on commercial speech: 1) a substantial government interest in regulating such speech; 2) a regulation that directly advances this interest; and 3) a regula-

101

tion that is no more restrictive than necessary. 55 F.R. 5185, citing <u>Central Hudson Gas & Electric Corp. v. Public Service Commission</u>, 447 U.S. 557, 564 (1980). But in arguing that its proposal <u>meets</u> these criteria, FDA discusses only the first two of <u>Central Hudson</u>'s three rules. There is no mention whatsoever of the third element, the requirement that the regulation be no broader than necessary.

The reason for this omission is obvious. FDA's proposal, with its requirement that all health claims pay obeisance to PHS-reviewed scientific and consumer health summaries, is in no sense "narrowly tailored to achieve the desired objective." <u>Board of Trustees of State University of New York v. Fox</u>, 109 S.Ct. 3028, 3035 (1989). To the contrary, the proposal could hardly be more expansive. It establishes an entire Ministry of Truthful Health Information within FDA, complete with curia (PHS), gospel (the Surgeon General's and NAS reports), and index of prohibited subjects (namely, anything outside the six FDA-approved health topics). Supposedly the masses (consumers) must be told nothing until this Ministry decides that it knows everything. How else can one explain FDA's mindset (not to mention choice of words) in threatening to punish those "who deviate inappropriately from model label statements and consumer summaries"? 55 F.R. 5183.

FDA "bears the burden of justifying its restrictions," <u>Fox</u>, 109 S.Ct. at 3035. Its attempts to do so, however, are little more than rhetoric. The agency states that it "wants to ensure that health messages are not presented in such a way that certain segments of the population will forgo

102

needed medical treatment based on the information they obtain from [food] label[s] ..." 55 F.R. 5178-79. But the agency cites no evidence whatsoever that this is a real risk. What data is there, for example, that discussions of the fiber/ colon cancer relationship on cereal boxes has led cancer patients to give up medical treatment for oat bran?

FDA rests much of its case on the supposed sanctity of the food label. It states that it "does not believe that it is in the public interest for the food label to lose its credibility" and it claims that "consumers view food labeling as more reliable and trustworthy than food advertising". 55 F.R. 5179, 5186. Under FDA's approach, however the food label encompasses everything printed on the food package — not just technical data on ingredients and nutrients, but Tony the Tiger too. Consumers will obviously view food label health claims in a different light than they do an ingredients list, just as they currently do not give uncritical acceptance to such food label phrases such as "Tastes Great!" or "New and Improved". Consumers recognize that food labels carry advertising as well as technical data, and that these two forms of information are not at all the same. Just as the appearance of Tony the Tiger on a cereal box does not make its ingredients list any less trustworthy, health claims would in no way detract from the credibility of the technical data on these labels. If children can tell them apart, why can't FDA?

FDA has also totally failed to meet the legal requirement that the cost of its proposed restriction on speech "be carefully calculated." Fox, 109 S. Ct. 3035. FDA repeatedly states its concern with minimizing the undocumented potential for misleading information from private speakers. At the same time, it is blissfully oblivious to the cost of restricting <u>truthful</u> information, especially in the one location where they are most useful to consumers — namely, on food packages. Prior to the rise of manufacturers' health claims, "government and general information sources were not effective in informing all segments of the population equally" about health effects. P. Ippolito & A. Mathios, <u>Health Claims In Advertising And Labeling: A Study Of The Cereal Market</u> xvi (Federal Trade Commission 1989). Such sources may look good on paper, but for many people they are useless.

The public health benefits of useful health messages are enormous. In its study of the cereal market, for example, the FTC found that the recent appearance of fiber/cancer health claims on cereal boxes had led to a significantly beneficial shift in cereal consumption, particularly among disadvantaged groups. See <u>id</u>.

The foregoing of health benefits such as this was the price paid by this country for FDA's prior policy of banning health claims outright. Under the reproposed rule, that cost will in large part be imposed once again. Moreover, scientific and technological advances will also be hindered by FDA's insistence on absolute certainty as a prerequisite to consumers receiving new knowledge. In its zeal to eradicate the possibility of misleading speech, however, FDA seems to be totally oblivious to the magnitude of these costs.

The logical result of FDA's campaign to eliminate the potential for misleading speech is to prohibit all speech; there would then be no possibility of anyone being misled, though of course no one would be very well informed either. But the choice "between the dangers of suppressing information, and the dangers of its misuse if it is freely available" is not FDA's to make. That choice has already been made by the Framers in favor of free speech. <u>Virginia State Board of Pharmacy v. Virginia Citizens Consumer Council, Inc.</u>, 425 U.S. 748, 770 (1976).

We submit that there is no legal basis for FDA's requirements of scientific consensus, of pre-approved scientific and consumer summaries, of mandatory cross-references to the latter on labels carrying health claims, or of mandatory nutritional labels in the presence of health claims. Such prior restraints have no basis in either law or logic. There is little reason, for example, to bar a health claim that expressly states that it is based on scientific data that runs counter to the prevailing consensus.

If certain health claims can be shown to pose a clear danger of public confusion, then FDA should consider a "split label" approach as an alternative to some outright ban. Under such an approach the claims would be allowed so long as the food label carried an appropriate counterclaim by FDA. If, as FDA claims, mandatory cross-references to consumer summaries will reduce the potential for misleading information, then clearly government counterclaims that appeared on the label itself would be even more effective in this regard. At the same time, they would be far less restrictive of speech than the total ban proposed by the agency.

The agency should also reconsider its opposition to private certification programs such as the American Heart Association's Heart Guide Program, which FDA recently succeeded in derailing. .See, e.g., "Heart Association Cancels Its Program To Rate Foods", N.Y. Times, April 3, 1990, at 1. Nutritional health issues are often complex, and many consumers prefer to use simple brand names or ratings, issued by organizations that they trust, as one guide to good eating rather than wade through the complex data on each food item that they buy. The availability of this option is advantageous, and the fact that it is based on expert opinion decreases the likelihood of individual consumer error. We gain by having the choice of using such guides as UL seals and Consumer Reports ratings when we make our purchases.

In recent years the same phenomenon has arisen in the area of food items, with certain brand names (Weight Watchers, Pritikin Diet) and food standards (such as kosher) serving an increasing number of consumers. The Heart Association's program had the potential of significantly expanding this system. By effectively vetoing it, and in the process probably eliminating the possibility of any other such program arising in the near future, FDA has crushed a legitimate form of communication. It has also done a great disservice to the consumers whom it claims to protect.

Rather than promoting "the societal interest in the fullest possible dissemination of information", FDA's proposed rule effectively destroys it. Central Hudson, 447 U.S. at 562. FDA should abandon both the rule and its interim ban on health messages, and adopt a policy of freely allowing substantiatable health claims.

Respectfully submitted,

SAM KAZMAN
General Counsel
Competitive Enterprise Institute
233 Pennsylvania Ave. S.E.
Suite 200
Washington D.C. 20003
April 16, 1990

Appendix 10: Congressional Directory

Congressional phone numbers and addresses. If you value your freedom of informed choice in health, nutrient supplements, and herbs, phone *and* write your Senators and Representative and demand that they support the Hatch Health Freedom Act. *Do it now, and do it often! Ask your friends and relatives to help, too!*

For the latest information on the legislative status of the Hatch Health Freedom Act — which will need your help *repeatedly* in order to get through Congressional committees hostile to freedom of informed choice in health — phone 1-800-226-4NHA.

Senate Phone Numbers, Offices

SR — Russell Building
SD — Dirkson Building
SH — Hart Building

Sample addressing:
Honorable Orin Hatch
U.S. Senate, SR-135
Washington, DC 20510

[same zip for entire Senate]

Vice President Al Gore.	224-2424	
Akaka, Daniel K., D-Hawaii	224-6361	SH-720
Baucus, Max, D-Mont	224-2651	SH-511
Bennett, Robert F., R Utah.	224-5444	SD-B40-2*
Bentsen, Lloyd, D-Texas	224-5922	SH-703+
Bidan, Joseph R. Jr., D-Del.	224-5042	SR-221
Bigaman, Jeff, D-N.M.	224-5521	SH-524
Bond, Christopher S., R-Mo.	224-5721	SR-293

Boren, David L., D-Okla.	224-4721	SR-453
Boxer, Barbara, D-Calif.	224-3553	SH-112
Bradley, Bill, D-N.J.	224-3224	SH-731
Breaux, John B., D-Lai	224-4623	SH-516
Brown, Hank, R-Colo	224-5941	SH 717
Bryan, Richard H., D-Nev.	224-6244	SR-364
Bumpers, Dale, D-Ark.	224-4843	SD-229
Burns, Conrad, R-Mont.	224-2644	SD-183
Byrd, Robert C., D-W.V.	224-3954	SH-311
Campbell, Ben Nighthorse, D-Colo.	224-5852	SR-380
Chafee, John H., R-R.I.	224-2921	SD-567
Coats, Daniel R., R-Ind.	224-5623	SR-404
Cochran, Thad, R-Miss.	224-5054	SR-326
Cohen, William S., R-Maine.	224-2523	SH-322
Conrad, Kent, D-N.D.	224-2043	SH-724
Coverdell, Paul, R-Ga.	224-3643	SR-204
Craig, Larry E., R-Idaho.	224-2752	SH-302
D'Amato, Alfonse M., R-N.Y.	224-6542	SH-520
Danforth, John C., R-Mo.	224-6154	SR-249
Daschle, Tom, D-S.D.	224-2321	SH-317
DeConcini, Dennis, D-Ariz.	224-4521	SH-328
Dodd, Christopher J, D-Conn.	224-2823	SR-444
Dole, Bob, R-Kan.	224-6521	SH-141
Domenici, Pete V., R-N.M.	224-6621	SD-427
Dorgan, Byron L., D-N.D.	224-2551	SH-825
Durenburger, Dave, R-Minn.	224-3244	SR-154
Exon Jim, D-Neb.	224-4224	SH-528
Faircloth, Lauch, R-N.C.	224-3154	SH-718
Feingold, Russell, D., D-Wis.	224-5323	SD-B40-1*
Feinstein, Dianne, D-Calif.	224-3841	SD-367
Ford, Wendell H., D-Ky.	224-4343	SR-173A
Glenn, John, D-Ohio.	224-3353	SH-503
Gorton, Slade, R-Wash.	224-3441	SH-730
Graham, Bob, D-Fla.	224-3041	SD-241
Gramm, Phil, R-Texas.	224-2934	SR-370
Grassley, Charles E., R-Iowa.	224-3744	SH-135
Greg, Judd, R-N.H.	224-3324	SH-513

Harkin, Tom, D-Iowa	224-3254	SH-531
Hatch, Orrin G., R-Utah	224-5261	SR-135
Hatfield, Mark O., R-Ore.	224-3753	SH-711
Heflin, Howell, D-Ala.	224-4124	SH-728
Helms, Jesse, R-N.C.	224-6342	SD-403
Hollings, Ernest F., D-S.C.	224-6121	SR-125
Inouye, Daniel K., D-Hawaii.	224-3934	SH-722
Jeffords, James M., R-Vt.	224-5141	SD-530
Johnston, J. Bennett, D-La.	224-5824	SH-136
Kassebaurn, Nancy Landon, R-Kan. . .	224-4774	SR-302
Kempthorne, Dirk, R-Idaho	224-8142	SD-B40-3*
Kennedy, Edward M., D-Mass.	224-4543	SR-315
Kerrey, Bob, D-Neb.	224-6551	SH-316
Kerry, John, D-Mass.	224-2742	SR-421
Kohl, Herb, D-Wis.	224-5653	SH-330
Lautenberg, Frank R., D-N.J.	224-4744	SH-506
Leahy, Patrick J., D-Vt.	224-4242	SR-433
Levin, Carl, D-Mich.	224-6221	SR-459
Lieberman, Joseph I., D-Conn.	224-4041	SH-502
Lott, Trent, R-Miss.	224-6253	SR-487
Lugar, Richard C., R-Ind.	224-4814	SH-306
Mack, Connie, R-Fla.	224-5274	SH-517
Mathews, Harlan, D-Tenn.	224-4944	SD-505
McCain, John, R-Ariz.	224-2235	SR-111
McConnell, Mitch, R-Ky.	224-2541	SR-120
Metzenbaum, Howard M., D-Ohio. . .	224-2315	SR-140
Mikulski, Barbara A., D-Md.	224-4654	SH-320
Mitchell, George J., D-Maine.	224-5344	SR-176
Moseley-Braun, Carol, D-Ill.	224-2854	SH-708
Moynihan, Daniel Patrick, D-N.Y. . . .	224-4451	SR-464
Murkowski, Frank H., R-Alaska	224-6665	SH-709
Murray, Patty, D-Wash.	224-2621	SD-B34
Nickles, Don, R-Okla.	224-5764	SH-713
Nunn, Sam, D-Ga.	224-3521	SD-303
Packwood, Bob, R-Ore,.	224-5244	SR-259
Pell, Claiborne, D-R.I.	224-4642	SR-336
Pressler, Larry, R-S.D.	224-5842	SH-133

110

Pryor, David, D-Ark.	224-2353	SR-267
Reid, Harry, D-Nev.	224-3542	SH-324
Riegle, Donald W. Jr., D-Mich.	224-4822	SD-105
Robb, Charles S., D-Va.	224-4024	SR-493
Rockefeller, John D. IV, D-W.Va.. . . .	224-6472	SH-109
Roth, William V. Jr., R-Del.	224-2441	SH-104
Sarbanes, Paul S., D-Md.	224-4524	SH-3O9
Sasser, Jim, D-Tenn.	224-3344	SR-363
Shelby, Richard C., D-Ala.	224-5744	SH-313
Simon, Paul D-Ill.	224-2152	SD-482
Simpson, Alan K., R-Wyo.	224-3424	SD-261
Smith, Robort C., R-N.H.	224-2841	SD-332
Specter, Arlen, R-Pa.	224-4254	SH-303
Stevens, Ted, R-Alaska.	224-3004	SH-522
Thurmond, Strom, R-S.C.	224-5972	SR-217
Wallop, Malcolm, R-Wyo.	224-6441	SR-237
Warner, John W., R-Va.	224-2023	SR-225
Wellstone, Paul D-Minn.	224-5641	SH-702
Wofford, Harris, D-Pa	224-6324	SR-283

+ Nominated for Treasury Secretary Dec. 10
* Temporary

Senate information.	224-3121
House information.	225-3121

House Phone Numbers, Offices

Sample Addressing}

[same zip for entire House]

> Honorable Chris Cox
> U.S. House, CHOB-206
> Washington, DC 20515

CHOB — Cannon House Office Building
LHOB — Longworth House Office Building
RHOB — Rayburn House Office Building

Abercrombie, Neil, D-Hawaii (11). . .	225-2726	LHOB-1440
Ackerman, Gary L., D-N.Y. (5)	225-260	CHOB-238

Allard, Wayne, R-Colo. (4)	225-4676	CHOB-422
Andrews, Michael A., D-Texas (25) . .	225-7508	CHOB-303
Andrews, Robert E., D-N.J. (1).	225-6501	LHOB-1005
Andrews, Thomas H., D-Maine (1) . .	225-6116	LHOB-1530
Applegate, Douglas, D-Ohio (18) . . .	225-6265	RHOB-2183
Archer, Bill, R-Texas (7)	225-2571	LHOB-1236
Armey, Dick, R-Texas (26)	225-7772	CHOB-301
Aspin, Les, D-Wis. (1)	225-3031	RHOB-2108
Bacchus, Jim, D-Fla. (15)	225-3671	CHOB-432
Bachus, Spencer, R-Ala. (6).	225-4921	CHOB-216
Baesler, Scotty, D-Ky. (6)	225-4706	CHOB-508
Baker, Bill, R-Calif. (10).	225-1880	LHOB-1724
Baker, Richard H., R-La. (6).	225-3901	CHOC-434
Ballenser, Cass, R-N.C (10).	225-2576	RHOB-2238
Barcia, James A., D-Mich. (5)	225-8171	LHOB-1719
Barlow, Tom, D-Ky. (1)	225-3115	LHOB-1403
Barrett, Bill, R-Neb. (3)	225-6435	LHOB-1213
Barrett, Thomas M., D-Wis. (5) . . .	225-3571	CHOB-313
Bartlett, Roscoe G., R-Md. (6). . . .	225-2721	CHOB-312
Barlon, Joe L., R-Toxas (6)	225-2002	LHOB-1514
Bateman, Herbert H., R-Va. (1). . . .	225-4261	RHOB-2350
Becerra, Xavier, D-Calif. (30)	225-6235	LHOB-1710
Bellenson, Anthony C., D-Calif. (24) .	225-5911	RHOB-2465
Bentley, Helen Delich, R-Md. (2) . . .	225-3061	LHOB-1610
Bereuter, Doug, R-Neb. (1)	225-4806	RHOB-2348
Berman, Howard L., D-Calif. (26). . .	225-4695	RHOB-2201
Bevill, Tom, D-Ala. (4)	225-4876	RHOB-2302
Bilbray, James, D-Nev. (1).	225-5965	RHOB-2431
Bilirakis, Michael, R-Fla. (9).	225-5755	RHOB-2240
Bishop. Sanford, D-Ga. (2).	225-3631	LHOB-1632
Blackwell, Lucien E., D-Pa. (2)	225-4001	CHOB-410
Bliley, Thomas J. Jr., R-Va. (7)	225-2815	RHOB-2241
Blute, Peter I., R-Mass. (3)	225-6101	LHOB-1029
Boehlert, Sherwood, R-N.Y (23) . . .	225-3665	LHOB-1127
Boehner, John A., R-Ohio (8)	225-6205	LHOB-1020
Bonilla, Henry, R-Texas (23).	225-4511	LHOB-1529
Bonior, Davis E., D-Mich. (10).	225-2106	RHOB-2207

Borski, Robert A., D Pa. (3).	225-8251	RHOB-2161
Boucher, Rick, D-Va. (9).	225-3861	RHOB-224s
Brewster, Bill, D-Okla. (3)	225-4565	LHOB-1727
Brooks, Jack, D-Texas (9)	225-6565	RHOB-2449
Browder, Glen, D-Ala. 13)	225-3261	LHOB-1221
Brown, Corrine, D-Fla. (3).	225-0123	LHOB-1037
Brown, George E. Jr., D-Calif. (42). . .	225-6161	RHOB-2300
Brown, Sherrod, D-Ohio (13)	225-3401	LHOB-1407
Bryant, John, D-Texas (5)	225-2231	CHOB-205
Bunning, Jim, R-Ky. (4)	225-3465	RHOR-2437
Burton, Dan, R-Ind. (6)	225-2276	RHOB-2411
Buyer, Steve, R-Ind. (5)	225-5037	LHOB-1419
Byrne, Leslie L., D-Va. (11).	225-1492	LHOB-1609
Callahan, Sonny, R-Ala. (1)	225-4931	RHOB-2418
Calvert, Ken, R-Calif. (43)	225-1986	LHOB-1523
Camp, Dave, R-Mich. (4)	225-3561	CHOB-137
Canady, Charles T., R-Fla. (12)	225-1252	LHOB-1107
Cantwell, Maria, D-Wash. (1)	225-6311	LHOB-1520
Cardin, Benjamin L, D-Md. (3). . . .	225-4016	CHOB-227
Carr, Bob, D-Mich. (8).	225-4872	RHOB-2347
Castle, Michael N., R-Del. (AL). . . .	225-4165	LHOB-1205
Chapman, Jim, C-Texas (1)	225-3035	RHOB-2417
Clay, William L., D-Mo. (l)	225-2406	RHOB-2306
Clayton, Eva, D-N C. (l)	225-3101	CHOB-222
Clement, Bob, D-Tenn. (5)	225-4311	LHOB-1230
Clinger, William F., R-Pa. (5).	225-5121	RHOB-2160
Clyburn, James E., D-S.C. (6)	225-3315	CHOB-313
Coble, Howard, R-N.C. (6)	225-3065	CHOB-403
Coleman, Ronald D., D-Texas (16) . . .	225-4831	CHOD-440
Collins, Barbara-Rose, D-Mich. (15) .	225-2261	LHOB-1108
Collins, Cardiss, D-Ill. (7)	225-5006	RHOB-2308
Collins, Mac., R-Ga. (3)	225-5901	LHOB-1118
Combest, Larry, R-Texas (19).	225-4005	LHOB-1511
Condit, Gary, D-Calif. (18)	225-6131	LHOB-1123
Conyers, John Jr., D-Mich. (14). . . .	225-5126	RHOB-2426
Cooper, Jim, D-Tenn. (4)	225-6831	CHOB-125
Coppersmith, Sam. D-Ariz. (1)	225-2635	LHOB-1607

Costello, Jerry F., D-Ill. (12).	225-5661	CHOB-119
Cox, C. Christopher, R-Calif. (47). . . .	225-5611	CHOB-206
Coyne, William J., D-Pa. (14)	225-2301	RHOB-2455
Cramer, Bud, D-Ala. (5)	225-4801	LHOB-131
Crane, Philip M., R-Ill. (8).	225-3711	CHOB-233
Crapo, Michael D., R-Idaho (2)	225-5531	CHOB-437
Cunningham, Randy Duke, R-Calif (51)	225-5452	CHOB-117
Danner, Pat, D-Mo. (6)	225-7041	LHOB-1217
Darden, George, "Buddy," D-Ga. (7) .	225-2931	RHOB-2303
de la Garza, E. "Kika," D-Texas (15). .	225-2531	LHOB-1401
de Lugo, Ron V.I.	225-1790	RHOB-2427
Deal, Nathan, D-Ga. (9).	225-5211	LHOB-1406
DeFazio, Peter A., D-Ore. (4).	225-6416	LHOB-1233
DeLauro Rosa, D-Conn. (13)	225-3661	CHOB-327
DeLay, Tom, R-Texas (22)	225-5951	CHOB-407
Dellums, Ronald V., D-Calif. (9)	225-2661	RHOB-2136
Derrick, Butler, D-S.C (3)	225-5301	CHOB-221
Deutsch. Peter, D-Fla. (20).	225-7931	CHOB-425
Diaz-Balart Lincoln, R-Fla. (21)	225-4211	CHOB-509
Dickey, Jay, R-Ark. (4).	225-3772	LHOB-1338
Dicks, Norm, D-Wash. (6)	225-5916	RHOB-2467
Dingell, John D., D-Mich. (16).	225-4071	RHOB-2328
Dixon, Julian C., D-Calif. (32).	225-7084	RHOB-2400
Dooley, Calvin, D-Calif. (20)	225-3341	LHOB-1227
Doolittle, John T., R-Calif.(4).	225-2511	LHOB-1524
Dornan, Robert K., R-Calif.(46)	225-2965	RHOB-2402
Dreior, David, R-Calif. (28)	225-2305	CHOB-411
Duncan, John J. Jimmy Jr., R-Tenn (12).	225-5435	CHOB-115
Dunn, Jennifer, R-Wash. (8)·	225-7761	LHOB-1641
Durbin, Rlchard J., D-Ill. (20)	225-5271	CHOB-129
Edwards, Chet, D-Texas (11)	225-6105	CHOB-328
Edwards, Don, D-Calif. (16)	225-3072	RHOB-2307
Emerson, Bill, R-Mo. (8)	225-4404	RHOB-2454
Engel, Eliot L., D-N.Y. (17)	225-2464	LHOB-1434
English, Glenn, D-Okla. (6)	225-5565	RHOB-2206
English, Karan, D-Ariz. (6)	225-2190	LHOB-1223
Eshoo, Anna C., D-Calif. (14).	225-8104	LHOB-1505

Espy, Mike, D-Miss. (2)*	225-5876	RHOB-2463
Evans, Lane, D-Ill. (17)	225-5905	RHOB-2335
Everett, Terry, R-Ala. (2)	225-2901	CHOB-208
Ewing, Thomas W., R-Ill. (15)	225-2371	LHOB-1317
Faleomavaega, Eni F.H, D-Am. Samoa.	225-8577	CHOB-109
Fawell, Harris W., R-Ill. (13)	225-3515	RHOB-2342
Fazio, Vic, D-Calif.(3)	225-5716	RHOB-2113
Fields, Cleo, D-La. (4)	225-8490	CHOB-513
Fields, Jack, R-Texas(8)	225-4901	RHOB-2228
Filner, Bob, D-Calif. (50)	225-8045	CHOB-504
Fingerhut, Eric D. D-Ohio (19).	225-5731	CHOB-431
Fish, Hamilton Jr., R-N.Y. (19)	225-5441	RHOB-2354
Flake, Floyd H., D-N.Y. (6)	225-3461	LHOB-1035
Foglietta, Thomas M., D-Pa. (11. . . .	225-4731	CHOB-341
Foley, Thomas S., D-Wash. (5)	225-2006	LHOB-1201
Ford, Harold E., D-Tenn. (9).	225-3265	RHOB-2211
Ford, William D., D-Mich. (13).	225-6261	RHOB-2107
Fowler, Tillie, R-Fla. (4)	225-2501	CHOB-413
Frank, Barney, D-Mass. (4)	225-5931	RHOB-2404
Franks, Bob, R-N.J. (7)	225-5361	CHOB-42g
Franks, Gary, R-Conn. (5)	225-3822	CHOB-435
Frost, Martin, D-Texas(24)	225-3605	RHOB-2459
Furse, Elizabeth, D-Ore. (1).	225-0855	CHOB-316
Gallegly, Elton, R-Callf. (23)	225-5811	RHOB-2441
Gallo, Dean A., R-N.J. (11)	225-5034	RHOB-2447
Gojdenson, Sam, D-Conn. (2)	225-2076	RHOB-2416
Gekas, George W., R-Pa. (17)	225-4315	RHOB-2410
Gephardt, Richard A., D-Mo. (3) . . .	225-2671	LHOB-1432
Geren, Pete, D-Texas (12)	225-5071	LHOB-1730
Gibbons, Sam M., D-Fla. (11)	225-3376	RHOB-2204
Gilchrest, Wayne T., R-Md. (1).	225-5311	CHOB-412
Gillmor, Paul E., R-Ohio (5)	225-6405	LHOB-1203
Gilman, Benjamin A., R-N.Y. (20). . .	225-3776	RHOB-2185
Gingrich, Newt, R-Ga. (6)	225-4501	RHOB-2428
Glickman, Dan, D-Kan. (4)	225-6216	RHOB-2371
Gonzalez, Henry B., D-Texas (20). . .	225-3236	RHOB-2413
Goodlatte, Robert W., R-Va. (6). . . .	225-5431	CHOB-214

Goodling, Bill, R-Pa. (19)	225-5836	RHOB-2263
Gordon, Bart, D-Tenn. (6)	225-4231	CHOB-103
Goss, Porter J., R-Fla. (14)	225-2536	CHOB-330
Gradison, Bill, R-Ohio (2)	225-3164	LHOB-1536
Grams, Rod, R-Minn. (6).	225-2271	LHOB-1713
Grandy, Fred, R-Iowa (5)	225-5476	CHOB-418
Green, Gene, D-Texas (29)	225-1688	LHOB-1004
Greenwood, Jim, R-Pa. (8)	225-4276	CHOB-515
Gundarson, Steve, R-Wis. (3)	225-5506	RHOB-2235
Gutierrez, Luis V., D-Ill. (4)	225-8203	LHOB-1208
Hall, Ralph M., D-Texas (4)	225-6673	RHOB-2236
Hall, Tony P., D-Ohio (3)	225-6465	RHOB-2264
Hamburg, Dan, D-Calif. (1)	225-3311	CHOB-114
Hamilton, Lee H., D-Ind. (9).	225-5315	RHOB-2187
Hancock, Mel, R-Mo. (7)	225-6536	LHOB-1024
Hansen, James V., R-Utah (1)	225-0453	RHOB-2466
Harman, Jane, D-Calif. (36)	225-8220	CHOB-325
Usstert, Dennis, R-Ill. (14)	225-2976	RHOB-2453
Hastings, Alcee L., D-Fla. (23)	225-1313	LHOB-1039
Hayes, Jimmy, D-La. (7)	225-2031	RHOB-2432
Hefloy, Joel, R-Colo. (5)	225-4422	RHOB-2442
Hefner, W. G. "Bill," D-N.C.(8). . . .	225-3715	RHOB-2470
Henry Paul B., R-Mich. (3)	225-3831	LHOB-1526
Hergor, Wally, R-Calif. (2)	225-3076	RHOB-2433
Hilliard, Earl F., D-Ala. (7).	225-2665	LHOB-1007
Hinchey, Maurice D., D-N.Y. (26) . . .	225-6335	LHOB-1313
Hoagland, Poter, D-Neb. (2)	225-4155	LHOB-1113
Hobson, David L., R-Ohio (7)	225-4324	LHOB-1507
Hochbrueckner, George J., D-N.Y. (1).	225-3826	CHOB-229
Hoekstra, Peter, R-Mich. (2)	225-4401	LHOB-1319
Hoke, Martin R. R-Ohio (10)	225-5871	CHOB-212
Holden, Tim, D-Pa. (6)	225-5546	LHOB-1421
Horn, Steve, R-Calif. (38)	225-6676	LHOB-1023
Houghton, Amo, R-N.Y. (31)	225-3161	LHOB-1110
Hoyer, Steny H., D-Md. (5)	225-4131	LHOB-1705
Huffington, Michael, R-Calif. (22) . . .	225-3601	CHOB-113
Hughes, William J., D-N.J.(2).	225-6572	CHOB-241

Hunter, Duncan, R-Calif. (52)	225-5672	CHOB-133
Hutchinson, Tim, R-Ark. (3)	225-4301	LHOB-1541
Hutto, Earl, D-Fla. (1).	225-4136	RHOB-2435
Hyde, Henry J., R-Ill (6)	225-4561	RHOB-2110
Inglls, Bob, R-S.C(4)	225-6330	LHOB-1237
Inhofe, Jarrles M., R-Okla. (1)	225-2211	CHOB-442
Inslee, Jay, D-Wash. (4)	225-5816	LHOB-1431
Istook, Ernest Jim, R-Okla. (5)	225-2132	LHOB-1116
Jacobs, Andrew Jr., D-Ind. (10)	225-4011	RHOB-2313
Jefferson, William J., D-La (2)	225-6636	CHOB-428
Johnson, Don, D-Ga. (10)	225-4101	CHOB-226
Johnson, Eddio Bernice, D-Texas (30)	225-8585	LHOB-1721
Johnson, Nancy L., R-Conn (6)	225-4476	CHOB-343
Johnson, Sam, R-Texas (3)	225-4201	LHOB-1030
Johnson, Tim, D-S.D. (AL)	225-2801	RHOB-2438
Johnston, Larry A., D-Fla. (19)	225-3001	CHOB-204
Kanjorsh. Raul E., D-Pa. (11)	225-6511	RHOB-2429
Kaptur, Marcy, D-Ohio (9)	225-4146	RHOB-2104
Kasich, John R., R-Ohio (12)	225-5355	LHOB-1131
Kennedy, Joseph P. II, D-Mass. (8).	225-5111	LHOB-1210
Kennelly, Barbara B , D-Conn. (1)	225-2265	CHOB-201
Kildee, Dale E., D-Mich. (9)	225-3611	RHOB-2239
Kim, Jay C., R-Calif. (41).	225-3201	CHOB-502
King, Peter T., R-N.Y. (3)	225-7896	CHOB-118
Kingston, Jack, R-Ga. (1)	225-5831	LHOB-1229
Kleczka, Gerald D., D-Wis. (4).	225-4572	RHOB-2301
Klein, Herbert C., D-N.J. (8)	225-5751	LHOB-1728
Klink, Ron, D-Pa. (4)	225-2565	LHOB-1130
Klug, Scott L., R-Wis. (2)	225-2906	LHOB-1224
Knollenbarg, Joe, R-Mich. (11)	225-4735	LHOB-1218
Kolbe, Jim, R-Ariz. (5).	225-2542	CHOB-405
Kopetski, Mike, D-Ore. (5)	225-5711	CHOB-218
Kreidler, Mike, D-Wash. (9)	225-8901	LHOB-1535
Kyl, Jon, R-Ariz. (4)	225-3361	RHOB-2440
LaFalce, John J., D-N.Y. (29)	225-3231	RHOB-2310
Lambert, Blanche, D-Ark. (1)	225-4076	LHOB-1204
Lancaster, H. Martin, D-N.C. (3).	225-3415	RHOB-2436

Lantos, Tom, D-Calif. (12)	225-3531	RHOB-2182
LaRocco, Larry, D-Idaho (1)	225-6611	LHOB-1117
Laughlin, Greg, D-Texas (14)	225-2831	CHOB-236
Lazio, Rick A., R-N.Y. (2)	225-3335	CHOB-314
Leach, Jim, R-Iowa (1)	225-6576	RHOB-2186
Lehman, Richard H., D-Calif. (19)	225-4540	LHOB-1226
Levin, Sander M., D-Mich. (12)	225-4961	CHOB-106
Levy, David A., R-NY. (4)	225-5516	CHOB-116
Lewis, Jerry, R-Calif. (40)	225-5861	RHOB-2312
Lewls, John, D-Ga. (5)	225-3801	CHOB-329
Lewis, Tom, R-Fla. (16)	225-5792	RHOB-2351
Lightfoot, Jim Ross, R-Iowa (3)	225-3806	RHOB-2444
Linder, John, R-Ga. (4)	225-4272	LHOB-1605
Lipinski, William O., D-Ill. (3)	225-5701	LHOB-1501
Livingston, Robert L., R-La. (1)	225-3015	RHOB-2368
Lloyd, Marilyn, D-Tenn. (3)	225-3271	RHOB-2406
Long, Jill L., D-Ind. (4)	225-4436	LHOB-1513
Lowey, Nita M., D-N.Y. (18)	225-6506	LHOB-1424
Machtley, Ronald K., R-R.I. (1)	225-4911	CHOB-326
Maloney Carolyn B., D-N.Y. (14)	226-7944	LHOB-1504
Mann, David, D-Ohio (1)	225-2216	CHOB-503
Manton,Thomas J. D-N Y. (7)	225-3965	CHOB-203
Manzullo, Donald, R-Ill. (16)	225-5676	CHOB-506
Margolies-Mazvinsky, Marjorie, D-Pa. (13)	225-6111	LHOB-1516
Markey, Edward J., D-Mass. (7)	225-2836	RHOB-2133
Martinez, Matthew G., D-Calif. (31)	225-5464	RHOB-2231
Matsui, Robert T., D-Calif. (5)	225-7163	RHOB-2311
Mazzoli, Romano L., D-Ky. (3)	225-5401	RHOB-224
McCandless, Al. R-Calif. (44)	225-5330	RHOB-2422
McCloskey, Frank, D-Ind. (8)	225-4636	CHOB-306
McCollum, Bill, R-Fla. (8)	225-2176	RHOB-2266
McCrery, Jim, R-La. (5)	225-2777	CHOB-225
McCurdy,Dave, D-Okla.(4)	225-6165	RHOB-2344
McDade, Joseph M., R-Pa. (10)	225-3731	RHOB-2370
McDermott, Jim, D-Wash. (7)	225-3106	LHOB-1707
McHale, Paul, D-Pa. (15)	225-6411	CHOB-511
McHugh, John M., R-N.Y. (24)	225-4611	CHOB-416

118

McInnls, Scott, R-Colo. (3)	225-4761	CHOB-512
McKeon, Howard P. "Buck," R-Calif. (25)	225-1956	CHOB-307
McKinney, Cynthia, D-Ga. (11)	225-1605	CHOB-124
McMillan, Alex, R-N.C. (19)	225-1976	CHOB-401
McNulty, Michael R. D-N.Y. (21) . . .	225-5076	CHOB-217
Meehan, Martin T., D-Mass. (5).	225-3411	LHOB-1216
Meek, Carrie, D-Fla. (17)	225-4506	CHOB-404
Menendez, Robert, D-N.J. (13)	225-7919	LHOB-1531
Meyers, Jan, R-Kan. (3)	225-2865	RHOB-2338
Mfume, Kwelsi, D-Md. (7).	225-4741	RHOB-2419
Mica, John L., R-Fla. (7)	225-4035	CHOB-427
Michel, Robert H., R-III (18)	225-6201	RHOB-2112
Miller, Dan, R-Fla. (13).	225-5015	CHOB-510
Miller, George. C-Calif. (7).	225-2095	RHOB-2205
Mineta, Norman Y., D-Calif. (15) . .	225-2631	RHOB-2221
Minge, David, D-Minn. (2).	225-2331	LHOB-1508
Mink, Patsy T., D-Hawaii (2).	225-4906	RHOB-2135
Moakley, Joe, D-Miss. (9)	225-8273	CHOB-235
Mollnari, Susan, R-N.Y. (13)	225-3371	CHOB-123
Mollohan, Alan B., D-W.Va. (1) . . .	225-4172	RHOB-2242
Montgomery, G.V. "Sonny," D-Miss. (3).	225-5031	RHOB-2184
Moorhead, Carlos J., R-Calif. (27). . .	225-4176	RHOB-2346
Moran, Jamss P. Jr., D-Va. (8) . . .	225-4376	CHOB-430
Morella, Constance A., R-Md. (8) . .	225-5341	CHOB-223
Murphy, Austin J., D-Pa. (20).	225-4665	RHOB-2210
Murtha, John P., D-Pa. (12)	225-2065	RHOB-2423
Myers, John T, R-Ind. (7).	225-5805	RHOB-2372
Nadler, Jerrold, D-N.Y. (8).	225-5635	CHOB-424
Natcher, William H., D-Ky. (2). . . .	225-3501	RHOB-2333
Neal, Richard E., D-Mass. (2)	225-5601	CHOB-131
Neal, Stephen L., D-N.C. (5).	225-2071	RHOB-2469
Norton, Eleanor Holmes D.C.	225-8050	LHOB-1415
Nussie, Jim, R-Iowa (2).	225-3301	CHOB-308
Oberstar, James L., D-Minn. (8)	225-6211	RHOB-2366
Obey, David R., D-Wis. (7)	225-3365	RHOB-2462
Olver, John W., D-Mass. (1).	225-5335	LHOB-1323
Ortiz, Solomon P., D-Texas (27)	225-7742	RHOB-2445

Orton, Bill, D-Utah (3)	225-7751	LHOB-1122
Owens, Major R., D-N.Y (11).	225-6231	RHOB-2305
Oxley, Michael G., R-Ohio (4).	225-2676	RHOB-2233
Packard, Ron, R-Calif. (48).	225-3906	RHOB-2162
Pallone, Frank Jr., D-N.J. (6)	225-4671	CHOB-420
Panetta, Leon E., D-Calif. (16)	225-2861	CHOB-339
Parker, Mike, D-Miss. (4)	225-5865	LHOB-1410
Pastor, Ed, D-Ariz. (2).	225-4065	CHOB-408
Paxon, Bill, R-N.Y. (27)	225-5265	LHOB-1314
Payne, Donald M., D-N.J. (10)	225-3436	CHOB-417
Payne, Lewis F. Jr., D-Va. (5)	225-4711	LHOB-1119
Pelosi, Nancy, D-Calif. (8).	225-4965	CHOB-240
Penny, Timothy J., D-Minn. (1). . . .	225-2472	CHOB-436
Peterson, Collin C., D-Minn. (7) . . .	225-2165	LHOB-1133
Peterson, Pete, D-Fla. (2)	225-5235	CHOB-426
Petri, Tom, R-Wis. (6)	225-2476	RHOB-2262
Pickett, Owen B., D-Va. (2).	225-4215	RHOB-2430
Pickle, J. J., D-Texas (10)	225-4865	CHOB-242
Pombo, Richard W., R-Calif. (11) . .	225-1947	LHOB-1519
Pomeroy, Earl, D-N.D. (AL)	225-2611	CHOB-318
Porter, John, R-Ill. (10)	225-4835	LHOB-1026
Poshard, Glenn, D-Ill. (19)	225-5201	CHOB-107
Price, David. D-N. C. (4)	225-1784	RHOB-2458
Pryce, Deborah, R-Ohio (15)	225-2015	CHOB-128
Quillen, James H., R-Tenn. (1)	225-6356	CHOB-102
Quinn, Jack, R-N.Y. (30)	225-3306	CHOB-331
Rahall, Nick J. II, D-W.Va. (3)	225-3452	RHOB-2269
Ramstad, Jim, R-Minn. (3)	225-2871	CHOB-322
Rangel, Charles B., D-N.Y. (15) . . .	225-4365	RHOB-2252
Ravenel, Arthur Jr., R-S.C. (1). . . .	225-3176	CHOB-231
Reed, John F., D-R.I. (2)	225-2735	LHOB-1510
Regula, Ralph, R-Ohio (18)	225-3876	RHOB-2309
Reynolds. Mel, D-Ill. (2)	225-0773	CHOB-514
Richardson, Bill, D-N.M. (3)	225-6190	RHOB-2349
Ridge, Tom, R-Pa. (21)	225-5406	LHOB-1714
Rocerts, Pat, R-Kan. (1)	225-2715	LHOB-1125
Roemer, Tim, D-Ind. (3).	225-3915	CHOB-415

Rogers, Harold, R-Ky (5)	225-4601	RHOB-2463
Rohrabacher, Dana, R-Calif. (45) . . .	225-2415	LHOB-1027
Romero-Barcelo, Carlos A., D/NPP-P.R.	225-2615	LHOB-1517
Rose, Charlie, D-N.C. (7)	225-2731	RHOB-2230
Ros-Lehtinen, Ileana, R-Fla. (18) . . .	225-3931	CHOB-127
Rostenkowski, Dan, D-Ill. (5)	225-4061	RHOB-2111
Roth, Toby, R-Wis (8).	2Z5-5665	RHOB-2234
Roukema, Marge R-N.J.(5)	225-4465	RHOB-2244
Rowland, J. Roy, D-Ga. (8)	225-6531	RHOB-2134
Roybal-Allard, Lucille, D-Calif. (33) .	225-1766	LHOB-1717
Royce, Ed, R-Calif (39).	225-4111	LHOB-1404
Rush, Bobby L., D-Ill. (1)	225-4372	LHOB-1725
Sabo, Martin Olav, D-Minn. (5)	225-4755	RHOB-2336
Sanders, Bernard, I-Vt. (AL)	225-4115	CHOB-213
Sangmeister, George E., D-Ill. (11) . . .	225-3635	LHOB-1032
Santorum, Rick, R-Pa (18)	225-2135	LHOB-1222
Sarpalius, Bill, D-Texas (13)	225-3706	CHOB-126
Sawyer, Tom, D-Ohio (14)	225-5231	LHOB-1414
Saxton, II, James, R-N.J. (3)	225-4765	CHOB-324
Schaefer, Dan, R-Colo. (6)	225-7882	RHOB-2448
Schenk, Lynn, D-Calif. (49)	225-2040	CHOB-315
Schiff, Steven H., R-N.M. (1)	225-6316	LHOB-1009
Schroeder, Patricia, D-Bolo. (1)	225-4431	RHOB-2208
Schumer, Charles E., D-N.Y. (9). . . .	225-6616	RHOB-2412
Scott, Robert C., D-Va.(3).	225-8351	CHOB-501
Sensenbrenner, F. James Jr., R-Wis. (9)	225-5101	RHOB-2332
Serrano, Jose E , D-N.Y. (16)	225-4361	CHOB-336
Sharp, Philip R., D-Ind. (2)	225-3021	RHOB-2217
Shaw, E. Clay Jr., R-Fla. (22)	225-3026	RHOB-2267
Shays, Christopher, R-Conn. (4)	225-5541	LHOB-1034
Shepherd, Karen, B-Utah (2)	225-3011	CHOB-414
Shuster, Bud, R-Pa. (9)	225-2431	RHOB-2188
Sisisky, Norman, D-Va. (4)	225-6365	RHOB-2352
Skaggs, David E., D-Colo. (2)	225-2161	LHOB-1124
Skeen, Joe, R-N.M. (2).	225-2365	RHOB-2367
Skelton, Ike, D-Ma. 14)	225-2876	RHOB-2227
Slattery, Jim, D-Kan. (2)	225-6601	RHOB-2243

Slaughter, Louise, M., D-N.Y.(28) . . .	225-3615	RHOB-2421
Smith, Bob, R-Ore.(2).	225-6730	CHOB-108
Smith, Christopher H., R-N.J. (4) . . .	225-3765	RHOB-2353
Smith, Lamar, R-Texas (21)	225-4236	RHOB-2443
Smith, Neal, D-Iowa(4).	225-4426	RHOB-2373
Smith, Nick, R-Mich. (7)	225-6276	LHOB-1708
Snowe, Olympia J., R-Maine (2)	225-5306	RHOB-2268
Solomon, Gerald B. H., R-N.Y. (22) .	225-5614	RHOB-2265
Spence, Floyd D., R-S.C. (2)	225-2452	RHOB-2405
Spratt, John M. Jr., D-S.C. (5)	225-5501	LHOB-1533
Stark, Pete, D-Calif. (13)	225-5065	CHOB-239
Stearns, Cliff, R-Fla. (6)	225-5744	CHOB-332
Stenholm, Charles W., D-Texas (17) .	225-6605	LHOB-1211
Stokes, Louis, D-Ohio (11)	225-7032	RHOB-2365
Strickland, Ted, D-Ohio (6)	225-5705	LHOB-1429
Studds, Gerry E., D-Mass. (10)	225-3111	CHOB-237
Stump, Bob, R-Ariz. (3).	225-4576	CHOB-211
Stupak, Bart, D-Mich. (l).	225-4735	CHOB-317
Sundquist, Don, R-Tenn. (7)	225-2811	CHOB-438
Swett, Dick, D-N.H. (2)	225-5206	CHOB-230
Switt, Al, D-Wash. (2).	225-2605	LHOB-1502
Synar, Mike, D-Okla. (2)	225-2701	RHOB-2329
Talent, James M., R-Mo. (2)	225-2561	LHOB-1022
Tanner, John, D-Tenn. (8).	225-4714	LHOB-1427
Tauzin, W.J. "Eilly," D-La. (3)	225-4031	RHOB-2330
Taylor, Charles H., R-N.C. (11)	225-5401	CHOB-516
Taylor, Gene, D-Miss. (5)	225-5772	CHOB-215
Tojeda, Frank, D-Texas (28)	225-1640	CHOB-323
Thomas, Bill, R-Calif. (21)	225-2915	RHOB-2209
Thomas, Craig, R-Wyo. (AL)	225-2311	LHOB-1019
Thornton, Ray, D-Ark. (2)	225-2506	LHOB-1214
Thurman, Karen L., D-Fla. (5)	225-1002	CHOB-130
Torkildsen, Peter G., R-Mass. (6) . . .	225-8020	CHOB-120
Torres, Esteban E., D-Calif. (34) . . .	225-5256	LHOB-1740
Torricelli, Robert G., D-N.J. (9)	225-5061	RHOB-2159
Towns, Edolphus, D-N.Y. (10)	225-5936	RHOB-2232
Traficant, James A. Jr., D-Ohio (17) .	225-5261	RHOB-2446

Tucker, Walter R., C-Calif. (37)	225-7924	CHOB-419
Underwood, Robert J., D-Guam	225-1188	CHOB-507
Unsoeld, Jolene D-Wash. (3)	225-3536	LHOB-1527
Upton, Fred, R-Mich. (6)	225-3761	RHOB-2439
Valentine, Tim, D-N.C. (2)	225-4531	RHOB-2229
Velazquez, Nydia M., D-N.Y. (12). . .	225-2361	CHOB-132
Vento, Bruce F., D-Minn (4)	225-6631	RHOB-2304
Visclosky, Peter J., D-Ind. (1)	225-2461	RHOB-2464
Volkmer, Harold L., D-Mo. (9)	225-2956	RHOB-2409
Vucanovich, Barbara F., R-Nev. (2). .	225-6155	RHOB-2202
Walker, Robert S., R-Pa. (16)	225-2411	RHOB-2369
Walsh, James T., R-N.Y.(25)	225-3701	LHOB-1330
Washington, Craig. D-Texas (18)	225-3816	LHOB-1711
Waters, Maxine, D-Calif. (35)	225-2201	LHOB-1207
Watt, Melvin, D-N.C. (12).	225-1510	LHOB-1232
Waxman, Henry A., D-Calif. (29) . . .	225-3976	RHOB-240B
Weldon, Curt, R-Pa. (7).	225-2011	RHOB-2452
Wheat, Alan, D-Mo. (5)	225-4535	RHOB-2334
Whitten, Jamie L., D-Miss. (1)	225-4306	RHOB-2314
Williams, Pat. D-Mont. (AL)	225-3211	RHOB-2457
Wilson, Charles, D-Texas (2)	225-2401	RHOB-2256
Wise, Bob, D-W.Va. (2).	225-2711	RHOB-2434
Wolf, Frank R., R-Va. (10)	225-5136	CHOB-104
Woolsey, Lynn, D-Calif. (6)	225-5161	CHOB-439
Wyden, Ron, D-Ore (3).	225-4811	LHOB-1111
Wynn, Albert R., D-Md. (4).	225-8699	CHOB-423
Yates, Sidney R., D-Ill. (9)	225-2111	RHOB-2109
Young, C.W. Bill, R-Fla. (10).	225-5961	RHOB-2407
Young, Don, R-Alaska (AL).	225-5765	RHOB-2331
Zeliff, Bill, R-N.H. (1)	225-5456	CHOB-224
Zimmer, Dick, R-N.J. (12)	225-5801	CHOB-228

Appendix 11:

The distinction between political speech (which the Supreme Court has afforded full First Amendment protection from government regulation) and commercial speech (which the court has sometimes held to a lower standard of protection) is not nearly as clear as might appear to be the case. The following are excerpts from Jonathan W. Emord, "Contrived Distinctions: The Doctrine of Commercial Speech in First Amendment Jurisprudence" (Cato Institute Policy Analysis No. 161, 29 pp, Sept. 23, 1991) Full Copies available for $4.00 from the Cato Institute, 224 Second St., S.E., Washington, DC 20003. Jonathan W. Emord is Vice President of the Cato Institute and a litigation attorney specializing in freedom of speech.

The Absence of Definitional Clarity

"Over the years the Court has moved from one obscure definition of 'commercial speech' to another, never adhering to a single definition for long. Before <u>Virginia State Board of Pharmacy v. Virginia Citizens Council, Inc.</u>, the Court found speech in the form of 'purely commercial advertising' not entitled to First Amendment protection. At times, it seemingly focused on the intentions of the speaker. Believing such intentions to concern the promotion of a sale, the Court held the speech in issue unworthy of First Amendment protection. At other times, the Court viewed the presence or absence of a profit motive as irrelevant, explaining that it would hold speech that did 'no more than propose a commercial transaction' to be undeserving of protection."

"In <u>Virginia State Board of Pharmacy</u>, the Court abruptly changed course. It finally admitted that commercial speech deserved First Amendment protection, reasoning that an individual's interest in commercial information 'may be as keen, <u>if not keener by far</u>, than his interest in the day's most urgent political debate.' But the Court failed to articulate a full justification for affording commercial speech protection. As a result, in subsequent years, the justices have had little difficulty in abandoning <u>Virginia State Board of Pharmacy</u> and reverting to a lower level of scrutiny for commercial speech. The Court has adopted an ad hoc, <u>content based</u> approach to deciding such cases, which has engendered as much confusion in the years since <u>Virginia State Board of Pharmacy</u> as prevailed in the years before it."

"When a representative of a private university, in a speech to a class of high school seniors, touts the academic and athletic curricula of the university in an effort to offset declining enrollment and thereby fill the university's coffers, is that speech commercial or noncommercial? The speech is profit motivated. It proposes a commercial transaction (enrollment and the attendant payment of tuition and fees). It concerns the economic interests of the university. It is a commercial announcement. However, it also disseminates academic information about ways to

125

better youths' educational and physical condition. Under the Court's highly malleable definitions, the speech is either commercial or noncommercial depending on the interpreter."

"When in a commercial announcement the president of an American automobile company urges people to 'buy American,' argues that by purchasing foreign automobile Americans are putting other Americans out of work, and states that buying his company's cars is a patriotic act, is the president's speech commercial or non-commercial? The speech is profit motivated. It proposes a commercial transaction. It directly concerns the economic interests of the speaker, and it is a commercial announcement. However, it also touches on matters of pressing political concern — consumer choice, protectionism, and free trade. Under the Court's many definitions of commercial Speech, the announcement is either commercial or noncommercial depending on interpreter."

"The definitional problem arises because almost all persuasive speech has direct or indirect economic consequences. We all spend the vast majority of our time engaged in some form of remunerative labor; hence, almost all speech encourages changes in behavior that produce economic consequences. In those substantive respects, the speech of the teacher, the politician, and the brush saleman are indistinguishable."